The Mwanawasa Years
An Analysis of His Presidency

Reginald Ntomba

Gadsden Publishers

P O Box 32581, Lusaka, Zambia

Copyright © Reginald Ntomba, 2016

All rights reserved. No part of this publication may be reproduced, stored in a retrieval system or transmitted, in any form or by an means electronic, mechanical, photocopying, recording or otherwise, without the prior permission of the publisher.

All photographs, including front cover, courtesy of Zambia News and Information Service (ZANIS).

ISBN 978 9982 24 1014

CONTENTS

Introduction		1
Chapter One:	The Eras of Transition	7
Chapter Two:	Chiwala's 'Export' to Zambia	15
Chapter Three:	Climbing the Greasy Pole	21
Chapter Four:	Old Ship, New Captain	31
Chapter Five:	The Circle and the Show	49
Chapter Six:	Battles Across the Divide	67
Chapter Seven:	Trying and Testing the Law	83
Chapter Eight:	Fighting the Cancer	89
Chapter Nine:	Governance of Laws and Lows	111
Chapter Ten:	Struggle for the Document	125
Chapter Eleven:	Searching for the Good Life	145
Chapter Twelve:	The Sinking Titanic	163
Chapter Thirteen:	One More Duty to Perform	171
Chapter Fourteen:	Reflections	181
Appendices:		187

INTRODUCTION

My first attempt at writing a book a few years ago went without success. In this business, as some may attest, you are not always lucky first time. I resolved to give it another try. This book is a result of that resolve.

I have read many books on presidencies, some of which inspired me to write this one. As a student of politics, it goes without saying that I love politics and power and their interface – but so far only as an observer and commentator. Politics is one of those subjects where everyone has an opinion. Author Robert Harris once said, "Politics is the supreme human drama".

When William Gumede, author of *Thabo Mbeki and the Battle for the Soul of the ANC*, was asked why he wrote a book on Mbeki, part of his response was that, "As Africans we need to tell our own stories." Gumede was right. It seems Africa is the only continent where anyone from anywhere can be an expert on it. This tendency has many times resulted in Africa being misrepresented by those who claim to know it better than its inhabitants.

Since we, as a people, elect leaders charged with the responsibility of charting our nation's destiny and managing its affairs, we should also be able to examine what exactly those leaders are doing with that stewardship. There are so many things leaders claim to do in the name of the people. While some can be given a benefit of the doubt, it's also true that others are only there to serve their own interests, never those of the people. It is for this reason that their record must be brought to light, examined and stored so as to afford future generations a chance to know where the country has come from, what type of leaders presided over it, what decisions they made and how such decisions affected the political, social and economic life of the country. What better way of storing such information than in books?

There is a serious lack of debate on books written in Zambia, particularly those on politics. There has not been sufficient debate and/or even challenge to some of the accounts presented, except for one-off reviews. In fact, much of the everyday political 'debate' is very shallow, ill-informed and sentimental, rather than rational.

The Mwanawasa Years: An Analysis of his Presidency

We must certainly increase our rate of reading and depth of analysis of issues concerning our country. We must not be frightened to criticise and praise as appropriate. Debate and divergence are the heart and soul of democracy.

There is currently not much analytical literature on Mwanawasa's presidency. This book seeks to contribute to the body of literature and public discourse on the matter. It discusses what I consider to have been the key events of that presidency. I have included information which is not specific to the Mwanawasa era to provide historical context to the subject.

In Chapter One I give a general background of the political phases Zambia has been through. This is intended to give the reader a glimpse of where the country is coming from. Chapter Two provides a brief background of Mwanawasa. Chapter Three discusses the events that preceded his rise to power. Chapter Four looks at the MMD as Mwanawasa found it in 2001 and how he led it after overcoming a bitter power struggle. Chapter Five focuses on the people who made up Mwanawasa's circle and what they did. Chapter Six discusses Mwanawasa's relationship with his political opponents. Chapter Seven delves into the failed attempt by the opposition to impeach him. Chapter Eight is about the subject that was the hallmark of Mwanawasa's stay at the helm – the fight against corruption. Mwanawasa carved for himself a reputation of a man who believed in good governance and the rule of law. Thus Chapter Nine looks at how he carried himself in that respect.

Each of Zambia's presidents has had to deal with constitutional reforms. Chapter Ten details Mwanawasa's approach. Chapter Eleven examines what he did on the economic front; where he succeeded and failed. Chapter Twelve explores one prominent foreign policy issue Mwanawasa dealt with and how his position on it differed from that of other leaders.

Chapter Thirteen ventures into the problems of leadership succession in general, but also with particular reference to the race to succeed Mwanawasa. Chapter Fourteen ends the book with some reflections on leadership and a summary of Mwanawasa's legacy.

Introductiom

NOTE: All the Kwacha figures used are in rebased form.

Reginald Ntomba
Lusaka, Zambia
March 2016

ACKNOWLEDGMENTS

In writing this book I may have sought information from other people in a bid to enrich it. However, all the interpretations and conclusions are mine alone. It's my considered view that I have attempted as much as possible to present the issues honestly and reasonably. But errors may indeed have been made. I carry the cross for those sins.

While I remain solely responsible for the contents, I inevitably accrued many debts in the process. My thanks go to Mrs Fay Gadsden and her team at Gadsden Publishers for being receptive to the idea and tolerating, firstly, my frequent reminders to approve the draft manuscript and, secondly, my request for a deadline extension as I pursued the various sources of information. Despite the long time it took to get the book completed, they stayed the course and supported me.

Special gratitude to my editor, Jenny Dodgson, for doing a wonderful job of it, for being both strict and generous, and for reminding me of some information that made the narrative richer. My thanks also to Nikki Ashley for proof reading the text.

There are several people I interviewed and others who gave me leads and provided me with information, some of whom chose to remain anonymous. I thank you all.

My friend Wilcliff Sakala read the entire manuscript and provided very useful insights, comments and suggestions that improved the text in many respects. Thanks dear brother for offering your time and intellectual capital to this product. It's yours too.

The long nights I spent writing would have been lonelier without my lovely wife Muzuwa popping in to encourage me and ask about progress despite her lack of interest in political subjects. Thanks sweetheart for being my only aficionado and for tolerating my numerous pieces of paper in the house.

Dedication

To Muzuwa and Austen

CHAPTER ONE

THE ERAS OF TRANSITION

"For Africa to me... is more than a glamorous fact. It is a historical truth. No man can know where he is going unless he knows exactly where he has been and exactly how he arrived at his present place." **Maya Angelou (1928-2014), American author and poet.**

BERLIN, THE FEDERAL capital of Germany, is a beautiful city. Its architecture is enchanting, its outdoor life entertaining. There is a café where politicians meet to engage in political gossip over cups of steaming coffee. If you want to know the latest political calculations in town, that café is the place to be. Berlin's art and culture is seen in stunning cathedrals, castles and museums with a rich collection of history and artefacts. It's also a great diplomatic centre hosting over one hundred embassies. The Russian Embassy looms large as it occupies an imposing 700-roomed Kremlin-style structure which resembles Zambia's intelligence headquarters, not surprising considering the southern African country's links with the Soviet Union.

Berlin has many histories within itself but two are particularly outstanding. Firstly, the Berlin Wall that divided East and West Germany was not only a physical wall, but an ideological one as well. That's why its fall in 1989 reverberated across the world – it was much more than just a physical fall.

Secondly, it was in this city in 1884 that European countries met to divide and share Africa into spheres of interest. Chris Bishop, managing editor of *Africa Forbes*, in a piece entitled 'Shame Stories Written in the Blood of Innocents', criticises "a bunch of old men with beards at the Berlin Conference [who] drew up the borders of Africa, with little regard for the people they carved asunder, for a continent thousands of miles away, in which most of them had never set foot."

In *Interventions: A Time in War and Peace*, Kofi Annan notes that "the

Congress of Berlin saw the colonial powers divide up Africa into territorial units that made no sense on the ground – partitioning kingdoms, states, and communities from one another, and arbitrarily melding others. Furthermore, the colonial system introduced laws and institutions that were designed to exploit local divisions to enable the strength of the colonial authority, rather than attempt to bridge these divides. It was these arbitrary boundaries and these divisive institutions and system of law that most newly independent African countries inherited in the 1960s."

Thus, except for post-colonial demarcations of Ethiopia/Eritrea and South Sudan/Republic of Sudan, the borders of most African countries as they are known today were drawn in Berlin. An entire continent was grabbed like a chunk of meat at a feast. For instance, Belgium's King Leopold converted the Congo, a country equivalent in size to the whole of Western Europe, into a personal property.

Through the Berlin Conference, colonialism came to Africa. History shows that the 1950s and 1960s were a particularly busy time for Africa. Africans had decided that time had come for colonialism and all its injustices to be banished and self-rule installed. During that time, various liberation wars were fought between colonialists determined to preserve the status quo, and Africans eager to break free from the yoke.

For Zambia, independence came in October 1964. The freedom fighters of yesteryear became the governors. So began another era in the life of a new nation called Zambia. Kenneth Kaunda, the first president of Zambia, led his fellow freedom fighters under the banner of the United National Independence Party (UNIP) in galvanising the people towards nation building. Zambians have much to thank those freedom fighters for.

A few years after independence, most African countries, including Zambia, adopted a one party system of government. Post-independence leaders reckoned that under such a political system, no time and energy would be expended on competing for state power and, therefore, all efforts could be concentrated on national development – the very essence independence was fought for. Another reason advanced was that a one party state would promote unity in a country and forestall ethnic/tribal divisions.

However lofty those ideas may have appeared in the eyes of the freedom fighters, they were altogether wrongly premised. It would seem they were more about preserving power than rallying a nation towards one goal. It is quite erroneous to assume that there's more unity in a nation under a one party system for instance than there is under a liberal democracy.

Valentine Musakanya (1932-1994) lived ahead of his time. He was Zambia's first Secretary to the Cabinet. He also served as Governor of the Bank of Zambia, Minister of State for Technical and Vocational Education, and Member of Parliament. His ideas on politics and governance were perhaps too radical for the environment in which he lived. In his appeal in the 1980 treason trial, Musakanya came up with a wide-ranging argument that included criticism of the one party state. The excerpt below is from his papers published posthumously in 2010:

> *When Kaunda realised in 1972 that UNIP had become a minority party against the combination of the ANC [African National Congress] and UPP [United Progressive Party] who together constituted 70% of the electorate, he then decided, contrary to his previous pledges to the people of Zambia, to turn UNIP into the only legal party. But the One Party State Constitution was overwhelmingly rejected when less than 40% of the electorate turned up to vote in the 1973 elections. The One Party System as it is today is not in the interest of unity but is designed to keep Kaunda and his cohorts in power for all times. Zambians are more united perhaps than any newly independent African country and they do not need a dictatorship to enforce unity. In any case, in diversity, there is greater strength.*

If there is one sin most African politicians are guilty of, it is that of overstaying their welcome. Africa has had leaders who were in power for as long as forty years. What would one be doing in power all these years?

Upon rising to the pinnacle, they espouse great ideas and preach selflessness. But with time, they cease to be leaders, they turn into rulers. Kaunda was in power for twenty seven years between 1964 and 1991. As stated earlier, freedom fighters should be given their due recognition for liberating the country from colonialism. But after twenty seven years, not even liberation credentials could save Kaunda and his team; the people had decided that they just had to go.

In 1960 British Prime Minister Harold Macmillan gave a prophetic speech in Cape Town in which he saw a 'wind of change' blowing across Africa. He was referring to the imminent independence of African states and his prophecy indeed came to pass as most African countries became independent in the 1960s. It was thirty years after Macmillan's speech that another 'wind of change' blew across the world. The Berlin Wall crumbled. The Soviet Union disintegrated. Another political era beckoned. In Africa the one party state with its associate ideology of socialism was overthrown and in came multi-party democracy.

By the late 1980s it was clear that the days of UNIP were numbered. A deteriorating economy, seen through increasing hardships for the populace, resulted in people beginning to revolt against the manner in which the country was being managed. In many countries, the price or scarcity of food has caused revolutions. The 1789 French Revolution was sparked by the escalating price of bread. So the issue of food prices (or the bad state of the economy in general) played a part in Kaunda's downfall, as did the constraining political environment in which personal liberties were heavily infringed upon.

In *End of Kaunda Era,* John Mwanakatwe, himself once a member of Kaunda's government, gives a highlight of the economic conditions that precipitated Kaunda's downfall.

Social discontent and unrest are often manifestation of a people's economic or political deprivation. The food riots of 1986 were spontaneous and widespread. The riots were not at that time necessarily an anti-Kaunda demonstration. Rather their occurrence was due to the reduction of subsidies on mealie-meal, the staple food of most people, which increased prospects of their families dropping below subsistence level. People were tired of endless appeals for "belt-tightening" in the midst of conspicuous consumption among the elite and widespread extravagance among the top UNIP leadership and civil servants in the country.

The tide of discontent with UNIP was irreversible. A pro-democracy movement was born in 1990 which led a sustained campaign for a return to an open political system. The suffocating environment in which dissent and other fundamental freedoms were suppressed was something that pro-democracy activists found unacceptable. There had to be a limit to which the masses could tolerate that suppression. Someone had to stand up and challenge the status quo.

Mbita Chitala and Akashambatwa Mbikusita-Lewanika have a special place in the history of Zambia's modern day politics. They were co-conveners of the Garden House Multi-party Conference that gave birth to the pro-democracy movement which was transformed and registered as a political party known as the Movement for Multi-party Democracy (MMD). This has been variously described as an act of bravery for the duo to have resolved to convene such a meeting in the face of Kaunda's intolerance for dissent.

"Totalitarian regimes were collapsing all over the world. We said we couldn't be left behind. We had suffered enough under the one party state," Chitala said when I asked him why he and his friend tempted fate by defying Kaunda.

The overwhelming calls for a return to multi-party politics made it inevitable for Kaunda and his colleagues to read the signs correctly, although some are said to have insisted that the pro-democracy campaigners were simply misguided and overzealous individuals who would be defeated. Kaunda had attempted to call for a referendum on whether Zambians wanted a return to multi-party politics. He was undoubtedly heading for defeat if he had gone ahead. His massive defeat in the general election exemplified the disaster that would have awaited him at a referendum.

But, to his credit, Kaunda did not resist the final call to leave. He has been praised for his magnanimity in accepting to cut short his presidency by two years in the interest of the people. Having won the 1988 general election, Kaunda's term of office was due to end in 1993. After amendments were made to the Constitution, Kaunda called a general election on 31 October, 1991 in which he was resoundingly defeated by the MMD candidate, Fredrick Chiluba who became Zambia's second President.

In *After Mandela*, Alec Russell recalls that in praising Frederick de Klerk for handing over power to Nelson Mandela in 1994, the British Ambassador to South Africa, Lord Renwick, remarked that, "The hardest thing in politics is not to receive power but to give it up." De Klerk's gesture was widely noticed as the Apartheid system had attracted global attention, but Kaunda cannot be denied his dues as he ceded power in a similar, peaceful fashion three years earlier.

Although it is said Chiluba was scared of attending the Multi-party Conference at Garden House Hotel for fear of incurring Kaunda's wrath, he cashed in at the earliest opportunity when he defeated Zambia's first Finance Minister Arthur Wina, lawyer Edward Shamwana and former Prime Minister and UNIP Secretary-General Humphrey Mulemba for the presidency of the newly-formed party at its first convention. In his book *Not Yet Democracy*, Chitala says that when Chiluba decided to attend at the last minute, he sat in the hotel car park, for fear of Kaunda's security agents pouncing, instead of going into the hall, until he realised that history would bypass him. This, therefore, is contrary to the popular myth that Chiluba 'brought democracy to Zambia'.

Then well-known for his trade unionism, Chiluba just happened to be in the right place at the right time. How he capitalised on sudden developments within the movement at the expense of its pioneers is a subject Chitala deals with at length in his book.

The Eras of Transition

Zambian freedom fighters, with their love for Mao safari suits, were replaced by a broad church comprising trade unionists, academicians, politicians, activists and outright opportunists. Commandist policies were discarded for capitalist approaches; economic liberalisation and private sector investment became the buzzwords. A new era dawned.

Given the hopes Zambians had invested in the new government, plus the goodwill handed to a group considered 'the second liberators', Chiluba had a great opportunity to move Zambia forward. Although he left a legacy of scandal, he deserves credit for a number of developments. His government instituted several economic and political reforms that were crucial building blocks for the latter years. He successfully moved to the private sector the once heavily state-run economy, although this was not without repercussions. Privatisation – the sale of hitherto state-owned enterprises – caused job losses. This subject is discussed in detail in Chapter Eleven. But the brighter side to liberalisation was the end of shortages of goods and services. What a relief it was. The housing empowerment programme that saw many Zambians own homes is another positive Chiluba is remembered for. The restoration of civil liberties that the UNIP dictatorship consistently denied the people was a direct product of an open political system in which Chiluba participated.

Chiluba presided over Zambia between 1991 and 2001. However he, too, nearly committed the cardinal sin, but the people 'saved' him – that's a polite way of saying the people rudely stopped his ambition of overstaying his welcome.

CHAPTER TWO

CHIWALA'S 'EXPORT' TO ZAMBIA

"Excellence is an art won by training and habituation. We do not act rightly because we have virtue or excellence, but we rather have those because we have acted rightly. We are what we repeatedly do. Excellence, then, is not an act but a habit." - **Aristotle (384-322 BC) Greek philosopher.**

THE SECOND OF ten children, Levy Patrick Mwanawasa was born on 3 September 1948 in the Copperbelt town of Mufulira. His father Patrick Mwanawasa was born in 1923 at Mukobola village in Chief Chamuka in Chibombo District, while his mother Mirriam Mokola was born in 1932 at Chapusha village in Kapiri Mposhi.

Some who knew him in his younger days say they were not surprised that he ended up in national leadership, ultimately as President. He was among the brightest stars of his generation. His leadership traits, they say, were noticed early at Chiwala Boys Secondary School in Ndola rural where he did his high school education from 1965 to 1969.

My search for Mwanawasa's friends and schoolmates led me to the Lusaka Central Business District where I tracked down veteran lawyer Humphrey Ndhlovu. I found him at his office on the bustling Cairo Road. Seated behind a mountain of well-labelled client files, perhaps reflecting his forty years at the Bar, he told me he knew Mwanawasa from his primary school days.

"I first met him at Fisenge in Luanshya," he told me as he searched his memory to recall the year, but to no avail. "His father was a businessman who owned a shop in the mine township. I was at Mikomfwa Primary School, while he went to one of the mine schools. As we were approaching Standard Three, we parted. He went to Fiwale Boarding School but we would still meet during holidays. When he went to Chiwala, I went to Luanshya Secondary School."

"He had a distinguishable personality and was a noticeable student," said

15

Mike Mulongoti, his junior at Chiwala."Besides being academically gifted, he attracted attention and respect and that is why positions like class monitor, prefect and head boy came naturally to him."

Mwanawasa's time at the University of Zambia between 1970 and 1973, where he obtained a law degree, saw his leadership credentials rise higher. "I knew him from university. He was very committed to his studies. On Fridays when most students would go out drinking, he would be in the library," evoked Anderson Chibwa, one of his close associates.

When students dismissed the entire students' union leadership for misusing funds, they appointed Mwanawasa to run the union singlehandedly. "He had a high sense of justice and integrity. Even fellow students he came with from Chiwala saw him as their natural leader," added Chibwa.

Ndhlovu and Mwanawasa reunited at university. "At campus, if you saw Levy then you knew I was close by, and vice-versa," he said, emphasising their closeness. Like other friends, Ndhlovu vouched for Mwanawasa's academic excellence. "He was studious, an outstanding student. He did not waste time doing funny things, he spent most of the time in the library," he recalled. "He was very approachable, he loved mingling and was willing to assist academically or otherwise."

High Court judge Eddie Sikazwe was Mwanawasa's senior at Chiwala and they reunited at law school. "I knew him as a friend. He was a considerate and well-focused person," he said. "That is why some of us were not surprised that he ended up as President. He was a team leader and believed in consulting." Sikazwe said that because of Mwanawasa's academic brilliance, his circle nicknamed him 'Judge Chomba' after the now retired Supreme Court judge Frederick Chomba.

Mr Injunction

From 1975, as he pursued his Bar qualification at the Legal Practice Institute (now the Zambia Institute of Advanced Legal Education, ZIALE) Mwanawasa worked part time for Jacques and Partners, who later took him on full time as

Legal Assistant until 1977 when he transferred to Ndola. When Ndhlovu, who shared a flat with Mwanawasa in Lusaka's NIPA area and later on Bwinjimfumu Road in Rhodes Park, heard of his friend's move to the Copperbelt, he ditched the Attorney General's Chambers and replaced him at the law firm, effectively launching a decades-long private practice. The two friends kept in touch and Ndhlovu made the line-up on Mwanawasa's wedding to his first wife.

In 1978 the future president formed Mwanawasa and Company. Seven years later, President Kenneth Kaunda appointed Mwanawasa as Solicitor General, a position he held for a year before returning to his firm.

Renowned for his courage, among the hot political cases he took on was the habeas corpus application involving then Zambia Congress of Trade Unions leader Fredrick Chiluba. "In the order of and scheme of things of that era, it was quite risky to undertake the defence of such a case. Levy, with me, took on that very unpopular cause and won – a very great feat in those days," reminisced lawyer Steven Malama at Mwanawasa's valedictory service in 2008. In 1989 Mwanawasa successfully defended Christon Tembo (former Army Commander and future Vice President) in yet another controversial case of treason.

Mwanawasa's legal expertise came in handy in the run-up to the return to multi-party politics in the 1990s. Although 'injunction' as a legal option had existed in the statutes for a long time, it had not been frequently used and Mwanawasa popularised its use as he often went to court on behalf of the MMD in its fight with UNIP in its dying days in power.

According to Chibwa, Mwanawasa had no intention of running as vice president of the new political party. He wanted to be chair of the legal committee, having already headed the same sub-committee. The general consensus was that at the first national convention, the National Interim Committee led by Arthur Wina was to be confirmed as the new National Executive Committee.

But, for all their bravery, the pioneers of the pro-democracy movement were beaten at their own game. In fact, they ended up on the periphery, while the newcomers entrenched themselves. "We were naïve and inexperienced. But for us we just wanted to bring change, positions were never our motivation," multi-party campaigner Mbita Chitala said, evidently satisfied with his place in history.

When it became clear that Chiluba would win, Mwanawasa talked to Wina to stand as party vice president because he believed Chiluba needed a strong deputy to keep him in check. Wina declined. Mwanawasa then moved to fellow lawyer Edward Shamwana, who had just been released from prison for his role in the 1980 attempted coup, but he too declined. Then Emmanuel Kasonde, who became Finance Minister in the first MMD government, told Mwanawasa that since he had identified the need, he should stand as vice president. Mwanawasa went for it and won overwhelmingly. In the general election, he was elected by a landslide as Member of Parliament for Chifubu Constituency in Ndola, before being appointed Vice President of the Republic.

At its formation, the MMD espoused great ideals. After eighteen years of one party dictatorship, the new party committed itself to a fundamental shift. Transparency, accountability, good governance and the rule of law ranked high. It was expected that these values would be translated into the running of government. It was not to be. By the time the MMD formed government, the project had already been hijacked by a cabal that was too focused on sharing the spoils. The pioneers and visionaries had been cunningly toppled by a clique that is said to have used both tribalism and other influences to run away with the trophy, entrenching themselves by grabbing the most influential positions in party and government. Mwanawasa was among those that assumed, perhaps too naïvely, that the team was reading from the same page and was about to do what it promised. But, as it turned out, he was among the first to notice that something was amiss.

It didn't take long for some members of the new government to start misbehaving and acting contrary to the great ideals and promises with which they had swept to power. Corruption and self-enrichment soon became their preoccupation. They had arrived at the stately table and they believed it was now their time to 'eat'.

"Sometimes Mwanawasa would come back from Cabinet meetings frustrated saying 'our friends are not in it for service'. There were ministers who were named in the Mwiinga Report as having engaged in inappropriate conduct. Mwanawasa told Chiluba to ask those ministers to resign. Instead, Chiluba went round to the culprits telling them what Mwanawasa had said," recalled Chibwa. "His frustration was building up. In fact, he would have resigned much earlier had it not been for some people like me and Henry Shamabanse who encouraged him to fight on."

It is apparent that Mwanawasa did not keep his frustrations to himself. Inadvertently, that prepared his friends for what was to come. "His main concern was that his colleagues were moving away from the realities. He was particularly frustrated that what they discussed in meetings was different from what was happening on the ground," said Ndhlovu. "On the day he resigned, he rang me at 2 a.m. and said, *'nafileka ifima* politics' (I have resigned from politics)."

On 3 July 1994, Mwanawasa resigned as Vice President, citing marginalisation of his office, insubordination from ministers and protection of erring ministers by the President. "Over the last two-and-a-half years I have found that there is a fundamental flaw between the inherent functions of the Office of the Vice President and the tools at my disposal to play a meaningful role in the realisation of our party's and government's aspirations," he said. "As a result of these embarrassing contradictions, I have as Vice President found myself in most embarrassing situations, where I have to defend decisions on which I am not consulted as an important member of Cabinet as well as an important political functionary."

Reacting to the resignation, Chiluba said Mwanawasa had on three occasions threatened to resign but he had prevailed upon him not to. A week before resigning, Mwanawasa told him of his intention to resign following then Health Minister Michael Sata's letter in which he berated the Vice President (more on this in Chapter Six). "I appealed to him to reconsider his position but alas the following morning I received his letter of resignation and I had no choice but to accept his wishes," Chiluba said.

In December 1995, Mwanawasa unsuccessfully challenged Chiluba for the party presidency after which he retreated from politics, back to private practice.

One can argue that it would be expected of Mwanawasa's friends and schoolmates to speak highly of him. But that doesn't disaffirm the fact that he had a colourful career with a stellar performance. His achievements in his earlier life only reflected the character, capacities and attitudes he would take to high political office.

CHAPTER THREE

CLIMBING THE GREASY POLE

"Leaders come and go; some last a few years, others several decades. There are several creative ways of "overstaying" in power. One thing, however, is very consistent: absolute, excessive and prolonged power can and will corrupt. Power blinds the correct perception of human dignity, justice and honour. This important point must be appreciated and internalised by all the political leaders, whether in the incumbent party or in the opposition bloc." – **Tesfaye Habisso, Ethiopian diplomat.**

IN LATE 2000 calls arose from within the MMD that Chiluba should stand for a third term. A third term is illegal as the Constitution of Zambia provides for two five-year terms only. Having been elected for a second term on 18 November 1996, Chiluba's time would be up in 2001. The only reason his supporters advanced for the proposed third term was that he needed more time to "finish the projects he had initiated". But others within the party argued that such a move would not only be illegal but also misplaced because the so-called finishing of projects was not tied to an individual, but to a system of party and government. In any case, they further argued, Chiluba had much earlier stated that he had no intention of outstaying his welcome.

According to Enoch Kavindele, Chiluba was not keen on seeking a third term but individuals who stood to benefit from his continued stay in power persuaded him. "I sat with Mr Chiluba and reminded him of his promise not to seek another term," recalled Kavindele, who served as Chiluba's last Vice President. "His answer was that the final decision would come from the Zambian people. If they asked him to, it was something he would consider."

In *The Long Sunset*, Vernon Mwaanga shares his attempt at dissuading his boss. "During one of my many conversations with Chiluba I reminded him that when we met at the Cathedral of the Holy Cross with Kaunda in 1991 under the watchful eye of Church leaders, it was Chiluba and myself who felt strongly that there must be a restriction as to how long a person could hold the office of Republican President. I made it clear to him that if he was going for a third term, then I was ready to part company with him immediately because I could not justify such a decision after what we went through in 1991."

When the third term debate gained momentum, Chiluba banned succession campaigns on the grounds that attention would be diverted from the smooth running of the party and government. He said this with all the pretentious genuineness he could muster. From a distance the reason seemed a real concern for 'family unity.' But it was not. Those closer to the centre of power knew the correct reading and it was nothing prophetic – Chiluba was spiritedly intent on succeeding himself. That was reinforced by the fact that all along Chiluba was not known to have placed his anointing hand on anyone, as the case normally is when a leader's time in office nears the end.

Interestingly, though, after the fallout, then Labour Minister Edith Nawakwi claimed at a rally in the capital, Lusaka, that Chiluba had promised her the mantle. But at another rally Chiluba denied owing Nawakwi anything. The revelation by Nawakwi – whether true or not – was meant to reinforce the view that Chiluba had promised to go when his time was up. Therefore, the calls for him to continue, and his ambivalence, could only be interpreted as a U-turn.

Party members were bewildered that a year before Chiluba's departure, the succession issue was still considered taboo. When the party should ideally have been talking about who would be its next leader, and by extension, a leader of the country, Chiluba insisted otherwise. But his hegemony did not go unchallenged. The first to publicly defy the ban was his own kinsman, Benjamin Yoram Mwila. 'BY', as he was popularly known, was the longest serving Defence Minister (1991 to 1997). Chiluba later shunted him to the Ministry of Energy and Water Development and finally to the Ministry of Environment and Natural Resources, moves said to have been aimed at frustrating him.

In his camp Mwila had, among others, Ntondo Chindoloma, the outspoken Member of Parliament for Chipili in Luapula Province, Joel Mwale, former

Ambassador to Japan, Chanda Sosala, former Ambassador to Namibia, Samuel Mukupa, the MMD's chairman for transport and Moses Kaunda, another member. After being subjected to the party disciplinary code, the group was expelled. This expulsion was expected to instil fear in other potential dissidents. But, as will later be seen, it did nothing to forestall the tide of discontent with Chiluba's scheme.

A fabulously wealthy businessman, Mwila formed the Republican Party and made a marathon tour of the country. He may well have been the most travelled presidential candidate in 2001 but he lost the general election dismally.

Chiluba sat tight and showed no signs of a leader headed for the exit. He elected to keep quiet in the name of 'encouraging debate'. But the so-called debate was all a sham because the only 'debate' Chiluba was interested in was that of his cheerers urging him on. If, indeed, he intended to promote debate, he would not have sacked ministers who opposed his scheme. Debate entails tolerating the alternative view, however unpleasant. On the other hand, if he had hoped that his silence would mean he was not interested, the opposite was true. His silence was too loud and only served to give impetus to his supporters to press on.

Pressing on, Chiluba tasked Paul Tembo, an eloquent party deputy national secretary, to go round the country with large sums of money to whip up support for the third term. If anyone had doubted Chiluba's scale of ambition, it was now becoming clearer. Many questioned why Paul Tembo allowed himself to be used in such a sinister scheme. Perhaps that was the depth of his loyalty to Chiluba.

Shall we part?
By early 2001 cracks emerged and in no time the rebellion in the MMD was out of control as more members openly differed with Chiluba. Senior Cabinet and party leaders such as Vice President Christon Tembo, party vice president Godfrey Miyanda, Legal Affairs Minister Vincent Malambo, Environment Minister William Harrington, Labour Minister Edith Nawakwi, Local

Government Minister Ackson Sejani, and deputy ministers Edwin Hatembo and Mike Mulongoti, among others, all stood against Chiluba's attempt to vandalise the Constitution. In one vivid instance, at Lusaka's Manda Hill shopping mall, Nawakwi reprinted and distributed copies of a newspaper in which Chiluba had promised to leave at the end of his term.

Chiluba was the chief dancer intent on continuing on the stage even when the orchestra had indicated it was about to pack up its instruments. He pushed the orchestra for a new song. But even the most illustrious dancer has a limit to which he or she can keep crowds spellbound.

The most spectacular development in this whole saga was that Chiluba was opposed and deserted by his closest and most senior party and government officials. It was quite a sight to see them address mass rallies to denounce their President. This show of defiance to a leader was unprecedented in the history of the MMD, let alone that of Zambia. But modern politics needs more of such. There should always come a time when followers show that they are bound by allegiances that are much broader and deeper than one leader's narrow interests. Those who opposed Chiluba, their other weaknesses and faults notwithstanding, showed their ability to stand for what was right at a crucial moment, even at the expense of their positions in the party and government and even at the expense of being denounced as disloyal. They refused to allow one man's tragic ambition to violate the fabric on which statehood is built.

Politicians so easily get comfortable with power that their downfall appears unthinkable. However, there is always a price to pay for failing to read the signs of the time. All over the world, examples abound. Michela Wrong, in her book *In the Footsteps of Mr Kurtz: Living on the Brink of Disaster in Mobutu's Congo,* narrates that Zaire's leader Mobutu Sese Seko assumed power at the young age of thirty five. He dominated for thirty two years and looted state funds to prolong his stay in power. But when the rebels advanced, his most loyal military generals told him to his face that they could no longer maintain peace in Kinshasa, nor guarantee his security. His downfall was imminent. Mobutu fled the country in 1997 and died in exile in Morocco.

Just as Mobutu's generals realised the hour of departure had come, some of Chiluba's political generals also grasped the limits of loyalty. They had decided that if Chiluba was going to sink, they would not sink with him. If there is one lesson to be picked from the manner Chiluba was opposed from within, it is that a leader should never think he or she has subordinates who are too loyal to rebel. Human beings in their innermost souls know where their loyalty ultimately lies.

As the MMD went to its convention in late April 2001 to elect party leaders, Chiluba kept the nation guessing as to his next move. He seemed to have enjoyed creating the suspense. Like the national Constitution, the MMD constitution provided for two terms only. But it was swiftly amended and Chiluba retained the party presidency unopposed, which in turn raised fears that he was up to some grave political mischief.

But on the evening of 4 May 2001, the same day the convention ended, he addressed the nation and bowed to pressure. "I will leave office at the end of my term. Let's take national interest in consideration. This is in the best interest of the nation," he announced to an anxious population.

The convention provided some drama. Even among members of the camp supporting Chiluba, some were duped. Paul Tembo was set to become the party's vice president and he reckoned, having done the dirty work for Chiluba over the third term, he would receive a handsome reward. Thanks to Chiluba's scheming, the position went to Enoch Kavindele. Paul Tembo was incensed and resigned from the MMD to join the Forum for Democracy and Development (FDD), formed by former MMD members expelled for opposing Chiluba.

To his credit, Paul Tembo did not deny his complicity in the third term fiasco. He apologised and described it as "the most challenging" part of his political career. Ever so tantalisingly eloquent, he spoke with a tone of contrition when he called a press briefing at Mulungushi Village, but I wondered how many believed him.

In politics, timing can sometimes be everything. At this stage his days were seemingly numbered. Paul Tembo was too much of an asset to the opposition considering what he knew and the role he played in promoting the ill-fated third term. His quick shift to the opposition was a huge gamble for which he paid with his life. On the morning of 6 July 2001, he was assassinated hours before he was due to testify to a Tribunal probing the MMD's theft of K2 million from Parliament – the same money he flew around with promoting Chiluba's unruly scheme. His death overshadowed the Organisation of African Unity (OAU) summit of heads of state in Lusaka. The opposition wasted no time in pointing a finger at the State as being responsible for his death, an accusation Chiluba dismissed as "very stupid."

The group of senior MMD members who fiercely opposed Chiluba remained estranged from the party. He particularly took offence that they teamed up with the opposition and civil society to publicly denounce him. He insisted they should have fought from within. But they argued that the matter was no longer a family affair as it hinged on the country's supreme law – the Constitution. Vindictive and known for being ruthless with people who crossed his path, would Chiluba ever forgive them?

Shortly after handing over the leadership of the African National Congress (ANC) to Thabo Mbeki in 1997, Nelson Mandela said:

One of the temptations of a leader who has been elected unopposed is that he may use his powerful position to settle scores with his detractors, marginalising them and in certain cases get rid of them, and surround himself with yes-men and women. A leader must keep the forces together, but you can't do that unless you allow dissent.

Chiluba found himself in exactly the same position. Re-elected unopposed, he expelled the twenty two senior members who formed the bulk of the party leadership. In addition, he fired them from Cabinet and replaced them with "yes-men and -women". Earlier, the twenty two had sought legal redress and tried to block the holding of the convention until the perceived breaches of the party constitution were addressed. But in his judgment, High Court judge Peter Chitengi was metaphorical in sending them back to the party when he said: "I would put it graphically that the cases that are before the courts are not the disease in the MMD. The courts do not have the medicines to cure the disease. The cure to the disease is with the MMD members themselves. It is, therefore, important that the MMD members meet to resolve these matters."

As Justice Chitengi refused to grant an injunction against holding the convention, the supporters of the third term went ballistic. I remember going that day to Kwacha House on Cairo Road, to the office of Michael Sata, then Minister without Portfolio and MMD national secretary. It was convention eve and delegates gathering there were in a carnival mood. Straight from court, Sata, puffing on his then trademark cigar, made a grand entry to wild cheers from party zealots. "I have just won my case," he bragged, as the crowd cleared the corridors to give their champion a smooth passage.

The third-term debacle, an artefact of Chiluba's political theatrics, was regrettable and remains a dark spot in Zambia's governance history. To Chiluba, it all seemed a thriller he enjoyed directing. But this misguided adventure and political experiment was to the detriment of the country and should never have been conceived in the first place.

Enter Mwanawasa - again

The MMD was deeply torn apart. Elections were due within months and the party had no presidential candidate, having frittered an opportunity to choose one at its convention. After all the chaos created by Chiluba, the party had to reorganise itself for a general election. Although the MMD managed to return to government by a slender margin, the third term campaign affected the complexion and popularity of the party. The MMD could not pretend that it remained the same. Two parties were born out of it months before elections. Former Vice President Lt. Gen. Christon Tembo led the FDD which had the majority of the expelled MMD members. Brigadier General Godfrey Miyanda, another former Vice President, formed the Heritage Party.

The MMD National Executive Committee started the process of choosing a presidential candidate in August 2001. Among the contestants were Vice President Enoch Kavindele, Presidential Affairs Minister Eric Silwamba, Minister without Portfolio Michael Sata, Mines Minister Chitalu Sampa, and former Finance Minister Emmanuel Kasonde. The so-called election that took place in the National Executive Committee was just a farce. By the time the five purportedly contested, Chiluba had not only already chosen his candidate but also secured his result. The 'political engineer' he prided himself to be, Chiluba dribbled his way through and installed Mwanawasa as the party's presidential candidate.

For many it was a surprise that Mwanawasa, who at the time was detached from both party and government and considering the circumstances of his departure from government, came into the picture. But Mwanawasa's former special assistant at State House, Jack Kalala argued that the perception that Chiluba "handpicked" Mwanawasa was not correct, because several individuals had requested Mwanawasa and suggested to Chiluba that the former be made successor.

"When I was Consul-General in Lubumbashi, I had talked to Mwanawasa about running for President. He invited me to his Teka Farm. I drove from Lubumbashi and picked up two other people on the Copperbelt and went to see him on 28 December 1998," an animated Kalala told me at a Lusaka restaurant. "We talked late into the night. My two colleagues pleaded with him and I spoke with passion and reminded him of his obligation to serve Zambia. But he refused."

Mwanawasa, Kalala said, told him his mother, uncle and wife would not accept his return to politics, especially after the near fatal road accident in December 1991. "He also told us he had become a Jehovah's Witness and his faith didn't allow him to participate in politics."

According to Kalala, several other people continued talking to Mwanawasa and he singled out former Community Development Minister Stephen Manjata as one of them, while former Western Province MMD chairperson Simasiku Namakando was said to have been among those who suggested Mwanawasa to Chiluba. Kalala remembers meeting Mwanawasa four times to persuade him and he eventually agreed with a caveat: "as long as you can convince my mother, uncle and wife."

Chiluba dissolved Parliament and set 27 December 2001 as poll date. Throughout the campaigns, he extolled Mwanawasa as the leader Zambia needed. By a minority 29% he won an election beset by various irregularities. His victory was later unsuccessfully challenged by three of the ten losing opposition candidates. Although Mwanawasa was declared winner by the Electoral Commission and later affirmed by the Supreme Court three years later, there is a widely held view that the MMD may in fact have lost the presidential election and barely hung on through the manipulative acts of incumbency.

CHAPTER FOUR

OLD SHIP, NEW CAPTAIN

"The idea that you can merchandise candidates for high office like breakfast cereal – that you can gather votes like box tops – is, I think, the ultimate indignity to the democratic process." **- Adlai Ewing Stevenson, American politician, 1900-1965.**

BEFORE THE 2001 MMD convention, the party president was the automatic presidential candidate for the national election. But aware of the political gymnastics Chiluba was engaged in, the convention, at his behest, changed that to allow "any member sponsored by the party." That was done for three reasons. Firstly, it was an exit strategy for Chiluba, in that while he would retain the party presidency, he would not be tied to the candidacy. Secondly, remaining as party president gave him an edge over the choice of the presidential candidate. Thirdly, being in charge of the party machinery would enable him to have a hand in government.

It was widely believed Mwanawasa would be Chiluba's puppet, thereby allowing Chiluba to continue governing from the political graveyard. What is true, however, is that the five members Chiluba bypassed – Kavindele, Kasonde, Sampa, Sata and Silwamba – were better placed to do his bidding. They were closer to him and would have towed his line more closely than Mwanawasa, who had been detached from the party and from Chiluba for seven years.

According to Mwaanga, "a majority of MMD members of the National Executive Committee and ordinary members held the view that the successor to Frederick Chiluba should come from among its ranks, to provide the kind of continuity which the party desperately needed."

If Mwaanga knew this, then Chiluba must similarly have been aware. So why didn't he settle for any of his close subordinates?

31

"He wanted a leader of integrity. He wanted someone who had not been scathed by corruption and scandals," opined Mike Mulongoti, a member of Mwanawasa's Cabinet. "If he had put anyone of those [who contested], they would have been lame ducks. Mr Mwanawasa was a brave fighter. He was going to withstand challenges."

According to Mbita Chitala, Chiluba told him he didn't have confidence in the people who surrounded him. "He told me he believed Mwanawasa could hold sway and unite the country," he said.

But some who were left out, such as Kavindele, felt Chiluba owed them an explanation for his decision to bring in Mwanawasa at the expense of other long standing members. After nine years, Kavindele broke his silence on the matter in a television interview: "It's not for me to say why I was left out and the other person [Mwanawasa] was chosen. That I'll leave to the memoirs of President Chiluba and I hope that one day he will have the opportunity to write his memoirs and he would explain. But that being the case I gave support to the person who was chosen."

Chiluba didn't live to write his memoirs. But in an interview with the South African Broadcasting Corporation on 19 July 2002, he explained his reasoning. "I thought that perhaps this will be a compromise candidate so that our nation does not get deeper into tribal divisions and that was the greatest crime to God and to humanity," he said, lamenting his fallout with his successor.

But when I interviewed Kavindele, he told me the intelligence had advised Chiluba that if the MMD were to retain power, it needed what they called a "neutral candidate" – close to Chiluba's description of a "compromise candidate".

"Forget about those others [who contested]. The leading contenders were myself and Mr Sata. But Mr Chiluba said he didn't have the idea of Mr Sata being President. He said he found him too abrasive," Kavindele told me as he paced around his Longacres office from where he worked on his railway project to connect the Copperbelt and North-Western Provinces. "To justify my exclusion," he added, "the intelligence told Mr Chiluba that I came from a minority tribe and that one or two provinces would not support me."

Taking Kavindele's version into account, then the intelligence assessment ran counter to Chiluba's idea of a successor who would unite Zambia across tribal lines. If saving the country from "deeper tribal divisions" was Chiluba's aim, why then did he pass over his deputy Kavindele and settled for Mwanawasa when both candidates originated from so-called 'small tribes'?

At the beginning of his term, Mwanawasa had asked Chiluba to stay on as party president, while he concentrated on running government. That was an innocent request. But he was seemingly unaware of its possible consequences. After the hiatus, Mwanawasa was something of a stranger to the MMD and many things had changed in his absence, but not necessarily for the better. Chiluba's supporters believed they owned the party and the interests of Mwanawasa and his supporters were therefore subordinate. As far as they were concerned, Mwanawasa was an outsider who had been favoured over the 'true blue' members of the MMD. Divisions between older members in support of Chiluba and the relative newcomers backing Mwanawasa made it a party of two halves.

Frustrated by the bickering, Chiluba stepped down on 9 March 2002. In a quick turnaround, Mwanawasa swiftly took over as acting president of the MMD. According to one senior member of the National Executive Committee at the time, Mwanawasa was advised that if he wanted to assert himself and gain control of the party and attempt to give it his character, he needed to take over party leadership.

However, Mwanawasa's installation was illegal. According to the party's constitution, in the absence of the president, the deputy would take over and in the absence of both, the national chairman was mandated to perform the functions of both. But who cares about what the law says when political survival is desperately at stake? In politics, at least as observed in the Zambian context, it's not always that the law prevails; many times expedience carries the day. It was said that Kavindele, then party vice president, was too preoccupied with preserving his position as Vice President of the Republic and therefore shied away from taking over the party presidency. But when I asked him why he, as the next in line, didn't take over, he said "the experiment" of having a different leader of the party and government had failed, as evidenced by the differences between Chiluba and Mwanawasa and he didn't want a repeat of the same.

The national chairman Chitalu Sampa was from the Chiluba camp and he was strategically bypassed. Allowing any of Chiluba's disciples to take over the leadership of the party would not solve Mwanawasa's headache because that leader would still be a Chiluba envoy.

In addition to the illegality of appointing Mwanawasa as acting party president, the National Executive Committee allowed him to act for three years, instead of the three months stated in the party statutes, after which an extraordinary congress should have been called. Mwanawasa's tacticians were keen to have him gain control of the party, and they were seemingly only prepared to call for an election when they were sure he had become rooted. So determined were they that they did it at the expense of their own laws. Thus, although Mwanawasa carried the reputation of a respecter of the law, this was one incidence where he did not quite live up to his reputation.

When the act defies the script

Mwanawasa's arrival marked a watershed for the MMD. Within three months, it was apparent he would not sing from Chiluba's songbook. When handing over power at the Supreme Court, Chiluba had said Mwanawasa would be "his own man". Possibly, Chiluba didn't know the exact consequence of his words, or he was merely saving face about the puppet talk.

Although there is a proclivity in Africa and elsewhere for outgoing presidents to retain party leadership, the incumbent generally feels more secure when he controls both party and government. No leader wants two centres of power – one of the party and another of the government. Where the former president clings to party leadership, fears abound that he may run a parallel administration and use the party machinery to frustrate the successor, especially if he refuses to fit in the ex-leader's pocket.

For instance, when Bingu Wa Mutharika succeeded Bakili Muluzi as President of Malawi in May 2004, the latter retained the chairmanship of the then governing United Democratic Front (UDF). But the two later fell out when Wa Mutharika launched an anti-corruption campaign which captured Muluzi and some of his former officials. Following hostilities between the two camps, Wa Mutharika left the party with his supporters to form the Democratic Progressive Party (DPP). The Malawian leader managed to change political allegiance at that high level without an election. The move plunged Malawi into a prolonged political stalemate between Muluzi's UDF and Wa Mutharika's DPP.

Even when it's not about former presidents, having a different leader of the party and of the government has been seen to pose its own challenges, especially if the leaders do not get along, or have different interests to serve. For instance, when Jacob Zuma defeated Thabo Mbeki for the presidency of the African National Congress at the historic Polokwane conference in December 2007, there were fears that the two would operate separately beyond the geography – Zuma at the party headquarters in Johannesburg and Mbeki at the government seat in Pretoria. Thus in his widely reconciliatory acceptance speech, Zuma had to emphasise that the country had nothing to fear as the two centres of power speculated about would not arise. But that was as far as it could go - assurance. Zuma was the hero, Mbeki was the fallen warrior. Divisions that had simmered over the years came to a climax with the unceremonious sacking of Mbeki by his party in September 2008, just eight months before his second term was due to end.

However, there has also been a counter argument that a President of the Republic should be left to concentrate on national matters and should not combine this role with party affairs. There is certainly no absolute position on this debate and it really depends on what works best in a given situation.

One of the major problems of political parties in Zambia (and elsewhere in Africa) is that they are built around an individual. This creates at least two problems. Firstly, it makes party leaders feel they are some kind of demigod that must be worshipped for the continued existence of the party. Secondly, it creates problems for whoever takes over, because it takes time for members to accept that the other leader is gone and they must embrace a new one and move on.

Mwanawasa was greeted with a hostile reception in a party where members were still reminiscing about the Chiluba years. He battled to legitimise himself and create his own brand of loyalists. While Chiluba's supporters were painfully coming to terms with the fact that their leader was no more at the helm and his influence therefore limited, they sought to direct proceedings their way. Since they considered Mwanawasa an interloper, they hoped they would still be in charge and he would be their puppet. As all this was happening, Chiluba was watching and there was no doubt as to where his support lay. At his first press conference after leaving office, Chiluba warned Mwanawasa's supporters that by displaying hostility to him and his supporters, they were "shooting themselves in the foot" because the government they were in was a product of the party – of which he was then leader.

Skirmishes between the two camps escalated, with Chiluba's supporters now accusing Mwanawasa of being ungrateful. But as time ticked, reality dawned on Chiluba's camp that their hour was gone and that Mwanawasa was in charge and their machinations against him would not work. Thus Chiluba's prophesy at the Supreme Court that Mwanawasa would be "his own man" had indeed come to pass. Another lesson on the African continent was delivered that the "Big Man" syndrome, where former heads of state want to control successors, does not work. When you give someone power and authority, forget about controlling them – they are effectively in charge. It was a classic case of succession gone dreadfully wrong. The outcome was contrary to how Chiluba had crafted the script.

"Chiluba and the MMD National Executive Committee must pay the price of waking up someone who was asleep at 02:00 am and offering him power on a silver plate, I actually mean a gold plate," Mwaanga scornfully reflects in his memoirs.

Was Chiluba surprised that Mwanawasa defied his script?

"If he was surprised, then he didn't know what he was doing. You cannot give power to someone you don't know. Power itself is a catalyst towards certain outcomes," Mulongoti told me at his office in Lusaka's leafy suburb of Kabulonga during a long conversation interrupted by phone calls from the media seeking his comment on various national matters.

Jack Kalala, who was a member of Mwanawasa's campaign team, shares that view. "I don't think he was surprised. As we were campaigning, it had started becoming clear that Mwanawasa would be independent. I remember at a rally in Livingstone where Chiluba and his ministers were present, Mwanawasa said Zambia had failed to develop because of inept, incompetent and corrupt leadership. We looked at each other with my colleagues in the campaign team but that was how bold he was."

Chitala echoes Kalala's view in that when Mwanawasa became candidate, he had his own small campaign team, separate from the national campaign team assembled by the party. "I was the campaign manager for the candidate. I told Mwanawasa that 'you cannot campaign with people the country knows as corrupt'. The idea of having our own team was to disassociate the candidate from the corruption of the past," he said, adding that Chiluba and his group were unhappy about it.

If Chiluba didn't see those flashing indicators, then it brings into question how well he knew Mwanawasa. Chiluba was in a very strong position to impose any candidate on the party and that was exemplified by the way he presided over the process, by summoning National Executive Committee members to his office and instructing them how to vote. But that he acceded to have Mwanawasa suggests that either he didn't know him well, or he thought he could control him or, as the common line goes, there were so many people vouching for Mwanawasa that Chiluba could no longer ignore him.

According to Kavindele, an unnamed member of the National Executive Committee had asked Chiluba if he knew Mwanawasa "very well". His response was that he knew him as his lawyer, as an Ndola resident and as a former vice president of the MMD and the country. Now, if that was all Chiluba knew about the person to whom he gave power, that was a huge gamble equivalent to testing the depth of the river with both feet.

"He regretted but it was too late. Mwanawasa had the instruments of power and you know what that means," Kavindele said, obliquely emphasising what someone with power is capable of.

In retrospect, Chiluba's gamble inadvertently gave the country another dimension of succession, politics and governance that would otherwise not have arisen had the script flowed as he had plotted it. It also gave Zambians a side of Mwanawasa they may not have known. It is the unpredictable events, the upsets and absurdities that give politics its drama.

On the turn-around by successors who may have been expected to play the puppet role, Agyeman-Duah notes that:

It is impossible to predict a successor's intentions and a leader can never tell how he will be treated once out of office. A subdued cat could turn into a tiger once it is freed and assumes the throne of the tiger. Leaders should therefore be careful what they do and how they exercise leadership responsibilities while in office. A leader must respect the rules that brought him into office and not seek to undermine them.

All of the above factors combined summarise Africa's leadership succession challenges and as long as they are not dealt with, the disgraceful tendency of leaders hanging on to power when they should be packing their bags will last much longer than is desirable for the growth of democracy.

Mwanawasa gained control of the party and diminished the influence of the so-called 'true blue', Chiluba loyalists. He succeeded in extricating himself from the tight corner he was in. If we are to re-examine Mwanawasa's request for Chiluba to continue as party president, it's unavoidable to ask: if Chiluba's supporters could give Mwanawasa a torrid time while he was leader, what more if Chiluba was still in charge of the party? Being surrounded by trusty members is of utmost importance to any leader and Mwanawasa was no exception. Having repelled Chiluba's brigade, he could now settle down and he quickly turned around the party leadership and ensured it was a new look comprising his faithful.

The wounded coalition regroups

Uniting the party and winning support outside MMD strongholds was Mwanawasa's longest political nightmare. After the election, the UPND controlled Southern Province. The FDD dominated Lusaka. Western, North-Western and Eastern were shared by UPND, UNIP and FDD. Therefore, the only provinces where the MMD won convincingly and could boast of support were Northern, Luapula and Copperbelt. But as fate would have it, these were the areas Chiluba's people controlled.

Chiluba and other reactionary elements, smarting from their loss of power in the party, went away disillusioned and launched an attack from outside to make Mwanawasa's leadership difficult in areas they commanded. Northern and Luapula were made 'no go' areas for Mwanawasa as Chiluba's supporters accused him of sidelining the two provinces based on tribe. Michael Sata and some traditional leaders daringly accused Mwanawasa of targeting his fight against corruption at the Bemba-speaking people. So, although Mwanawasa had managed to get the National Executive Committee under his control, winning opposition camps and asserting himself in areas controlled by Chiluba was a tricky affair.

Revenge lurked on the horizon. In the 2006 election, Chiluba and his supporters regrouped and rallied around Sata, the leader and presidential candidate of the Patriotic Front. In a last ditch effort to control the tide ahead of balloting in a few weeks' time, Chiluba, on return from medical treatment in South Africa, publicly praised and endorsed Sata. But this was the same person he had passed over five years earlier. That historical fact was irrelevant to both of them. Chiluba was only eager to use Sata's Patriotic Front as his newly-found political vehicle to flay Mwanawasa following their spectacular fallout.

The Patriotic Front used everything they could to alienate Mwanawasa from Northern and Luapula voters. Chiluba's trouble with the law turned out to be a grand political feast which they exploited to stupendous effect. They energetically fronted Chiluba's prosecution as an enormous act of ingratitude and betrayal by Mwanawasa. They advanced the notion that by initiating

Chiluba's arrest, Mwanawasa had effectively forfeited the Northern and Luapula vote. With Chiluba's supporters retaining a thick political muscle in the two provinces, Mwanawasa had no hope. That may well explain why he did not spend much time there appealing for votes he apparently knew would not come.

Sata had struck gold. A wily and proficient politician, he realised just what an asset Chiluba's legal baggage was to his electoral fortunes. Sensing the imminent landslide in Northern and Luapula, he steamed his campaign wagon there and dangled the infamous carrot by openly pledging to stop Chiluba's prosecution if he won. The catch was clear: Chiluba hailed from Luapula where he retained overwhelming sympathy. So why would Chiluba's supporters in Northern and Luapula not shore up a man who had promised to shred his indictment? With emotions running high and propaganda marshalled against Mwanawasa, only a miracle could save him in Northern and Luapula, because the message that he had betrayed Chiluba 'our son' had sunk deep.

However, Chiluba's arrest and subsequent prosecution had nothing to do with lack of loyalty by Mwanawasa. Sata was just seeking political capital out of Chiluba's inconvenience with the law. It is not that he believed Chiluba was innocent; it was all about using him for electoral gain. For Chiluba he was sure he had found political sanctuary in the Patriotic Front. It was all about using Sata to get out of Mwanawasa's dragnet. That is why when Chiluba decamped from the Patriotic Front to return to MMD after Mwanawasa's death, Sata immediately voiced his true position on Chiluba. In all, that brief 'come together' was only a web of hard survival, great deceit and sheer opportunism. Sata managed to win votes by inflaming the passions of Chiluba's sympathisers. That opportunistic move was, however costly and brought to light exactly where he stood on corruption. Sata was prepared to interfere with judicial processes to advance his political interests. Would he respect the judiciary if he came to power?

As the results of the general election poured in, Sata swept the votes in Northern, Luapula, Lusaka and Copperbelt. His political charisma and his promises – mainly tax reform – charmed the disenchanted urban dwellers, while in Northern and Luapula Sata's own popularity and the Chiluba factor weighed in. Chiluba was not alone in seeking solace in the Patriotic Front. His followers also flocked there and formed the bulk of the forty two parliamentary seats Sata got, a massive increase from only one in 2001.

Mwanawasa made massive gains in former opposition territories such as North-Western, Western and Eastern Provinces, but elsewhere he paid a high premium for taking the unpopular path of prosecuting Chiluba. Like Kennedy who declared his readiness to lose re-election for advancing civil rights, Mwanawasa repeatedly declared his willingness to lose the Presidency for fighting corruption.

The election also brought Mwanawasa's leadership to test in at least two ways. Firstly, unlike in 2001 when Chiluba campaigned for him, this time Mwanawasa took to the platform to defend his record and prove to the voters that he deserved another term. Secondly, he was up against a resurgent opposition that was once part of his party. Would they get him out of power using the same means they got him there? Even more interesting was that the man who extolled him and handed him the Presidency had joined the opposition. This must have increased Mwanawasa's insecurities.

A tale of two tales

Chiluba and Mwanawasa couldn't have been more different. Chiluba was a populist who clearly enjoyed the political game. He easily identified with the grassroots, spoke their language and went to great lengths to appease them. Party supporters enjoyed his unfettered patronage. They ran markets and bus stations and pocketed levies. Although even in the Second Republic UNIP controlled markets, its members could have perhaps misconstrued their being the only political party to mean they could be so overbearing. But in a plural political set up, to have a party controlling markets and bus stations and collecting levies in the name of the party was out of step with the political dispensation of the time and an illegality, as this remains the sole responsibility of municipal authorities. (Unfortunately, this trend continues today despite the Markets and Bus Stations Act empowering municipalities to take charge).

Chiluba created for party members what he called a 'Vendors Desk' at State House and assigned it a Deputy Minister. Much to their liking, he said vendors were "part of the Office of the President." It is, however, not known what benefits accrued to the country by virtue of that creation. The Vendors' Desk was just a centre for markets and bus station branches of the MMD, another example of Chiluba's populist appeasement of party supporters. Perhaps that said much about his worldview of the Presidency.

Mwanawasa's approach was different. He bluntly told party members he was not in the habit of dishing out money. That position was consistent with his high profile fight against corruption. It would be contradictory to have a President proclaiming repugnance for misuse of public funds and then dip in the national treasury to excite supporters. He entertained them when they marched to State House to "show solidarity", but he didn't go to Chiluba's bountiful levels of 'generosity'. They noticed the difference and complaints arose of how infrequently they were entertained, funded and feted at State House.

The difference in the disposition of the two could in part be explained by their backgrounds. Chiluba's trade union experience made him better at public relations. Silver-tongued and at home with crowds, that simply made him a professional politician. He waxed lyrical and was always comfy engaging in retail politics. But Mwanawasa was not a politician in the populist mould, he struggled and appeared awkward on the political podium. A lawyer accustomed to a strict and defined way of doing things, he remained a guest in the messier negotiations of politics. He was more at ease in the courtroom: his interaction with the public was therefore limited. That explained his aloofness.

Chiluba quoted Machiavelli and Hobbes to burnish his Warwick credentials; Mwanawasa had no time for philosophising, he was a straight-to-the-point type. From his humble background, Chiluba was involved in an endless task of self-remodelling –a fighter for workers' rights, an anti-socialist, a self-acclaimed democrat and Pan-Africanist, a charismatic Christian, and, never to be missed, flamboyant to all intents and purposes. The latter may explain his opulent and vast wardrobe which eventually included one hundred pairs of shoes, three hudred shirts and one hundred and fifty suits. Mwanawasa remained who he was, simply a lawyer comfortable in his skin without ostentation.

Having worked with both leaders, Mwaanga shares his contrasts between the two leaders. On Chiluba, he says:

He had an informal style of government and although Cabinet meetings sometimes started late, they actually ran on time most of the time. He developed a personal relationship with his ministers in that when he heard something adverse about a particular minister, he called him or her to his office and talked to that minister and as a result, ministers developed a sense of respect for the President they worked for. When ministers had bereavements, he visited their homes, telephoned them at home and gave them comfort and this created a strong bond between him and his ministers. He was somewhat secretive about certain things which were going on and he worked long hours to try and get the country moving forward.

Mwanawasa, Mwaanga says, "brought a totally different culture to government. Cabinet meetings almost never started on time. His relationship with his ministers was very distant. He was highly emotional, impulsive and had a very short temper. Ministers were literally terrified of their President and each time there was a private discussion among ministers, this dominated discussion."

Former Cabinet minister and Kaputa legislator Mutale Nalumango says while Mwanawasa was a tough disciplinarian, he gave his ministers space to work. "He was not a jack of all trades, he allowed ministers to do their job," she held. "What I knew of him also is that he was not double-tongued. What he told you in private is what he would say in public. He had no time for gossip."

Consistent with his dislike for gossip, he had a habit of challenging people who took allegations to him. Tourism Minister Kabinga Pande recalled a time when some people reported to Mwanawasa that he, Pande was engaged in corruption. "Six months later he called the same people and asked them to specify and provide evidence of the corruption I was supposedly involved in. They failed and he told them he knew I was not involved in such things."

For those who worked with Mwanawasa, it was apparently difficult to pretend they didn't know what the President wanted of them. Their in-trays were a constant reminder, an example of how Mwanawasa succeeded in imposing his own order and procedure on the operations of government. "I would find about twenty letters in one day. We told him, 'Mr President, we are not running a law firm'," said Kavindele.

"I do not think we shall have another President who will excel better than President Mwanawasa at letter writing. There were times I would find three to four very well crafted letters on my desk in one day concerning issues which would have been sorted out using just one ten-minute telephone conversation," recalls Mwaanga.

When he was visiting his Mpongwe constituency, Gabriel Namulambe publicly castigated the Road Development Agency for not working on the Mpongwe-Machiya Road. Mwanawasa saw him on TV. "When I returned to Lusaka I found a letter of final warning admonishing me for attacking an arm of government under the supervision of my counterpart at Works and Supply," revealed Namulambe."He was a disciplinarian, he told me the failure to work on that road was collective as government and I could not be seen in public attacking my colleague in that fashion."

Family battles resurface
As party leader from 2002, Mwanawasa had had a relatively easy time. It was not until three years later that he got his first major test. Provincial party conventions declared him "the sole presidential candidate" ahead of the national convention, an early warning that his supporters would not tolerate challengers. This was embarrassing for a party that criticised UNIP elections where Kaunda 'contested' alone. Instead of opening the democratic space, Mwanawasa's supporters were doing everything to reduce it to levels where opponents were ostracised and accused of being disloyal. In many political

parties there seems to be a gross misunderstanding of what 'disloyalty' means. It seems challenging the incumbent is the greatest mark of disloyalty. What many do not know, however, is that you can choose not to challenge the incumbent but still undermine him or her in a much more grievous manner.

Mwanawasa's supporters did everything to frustrate challengers. Mwaanga, then party national secretary, said there was an "unwritten rule" that no one could challenge the incumbent. By revealing the "unwritten rule" the party – knowingly or otherwise – made it plain that the real reason for haranguing Mwanawasa's rivals was not because they had flouted any law but because they had exhibited their ambitions at the wrong time.

Despite such undemocratic antics challengers began to emerge, including Nason Msoni who had led the little known Labour Party and later joined the MMD, and Mwaba Mushota, another member of the party. But they had no constituency and thus stood no chance whatsoever. As the duo posed no threat to the king, the royal guards were at peace.

However, what appeared a credible challenge came from former Vice President Nevers Mumba. A famous televangelist turned politician, Mumba abandoned his party, National Citizens Coalition, to accept an appointment as Mwanawasa's deputy. He served for sixteen months and got fired after a diplomatic gaffe. While acting as President, Mumba made a statement to the media, accusing unnamed figures in the neighbouring Democratic Republic of Congo of supporting the opposition in Zambia.

Mumba's candidature apparently created ripples in the party and raised the temperature to another level. Mwanawasa's supporters swung into action. But Nalumango argued that Mumba's popularity was exaggerated. "He was never a factor in MMD. He was a stranger who was brought in by President Mwanawasa. I can tell you that as politicians we all purport to be influential, but he was not a factor."

Despite Mwanawasa repeatedly declaring his readiness to be challenged, the manner his supporters – with or without his blessings – dealt with opposition polluted intra-party democracy. They accused Mumba of being ungrateful for his appointment as Vice President. When I put it to Nalumango that Mwanawasa's supporters were rather drastic with Mumba, her response was: "That's politics. Mwanawasa's supporters wanted him to win. Mumba's supporters wanted Mumba to win. It was a competition."

Mumba announced his candidature on 18 March 2005 for a convention initially scheduled for May but later pushed to July. On 31 May, he was expelled for "gross indiscipline and disregarding the disciplinary code." His attempt to seek redress in the courts failed. The party gave other obscure reasons for postponing the convention from May to July, but it was clear that the interim was meant to exclude Mumba.

The build-up to the convention had threatened to rip the party apart. There were camps within a camp, tension was high and the campaigns were as intense as they were divisive. Success in the general elections depended on how the party would emerge from that process of internal democracy.

Serious allegations of corruption emerged prior to the convention. Mumba accused Mwanawasa and his agents of engaging in corruption to win. In reaction, the party appointed a seven-member tribunal to probe the allegations. Mumba handed in a chunk of documentation to argue his case. But the tribunal cleared Mwanawasa on grounds that Mumba's dossier did not link Mwanawasa to the alleged corruption. Assuming Mwanawasa had been found wanting, would the tribunal have gathered the courage to say so? There were some members who thought Mwanawasa didn't even know what was happening and if there was any corruption, it was his supporters who were being overzealous. If true, that would be explained by Mwanawasa's detachment from the hard-core party politics. But others held the view that the tribunal was just a smokescreen. The tribunal, however, reprimanded senior members like Mwaanga and Daniel Munkombwe.

With Mumba dealt with, Mwanawasa's victory was a foregone conclusion but not before Kavindele staged another insignificant challenge; he was trounced with sixty eight votes against Mwanawasa's runaway 1,211 votes. Mwanawasa was as good as "the sole presidential candidate" he had been declared by the provinces. But what did his victory contribute to intraparty democracy? Most, if not all, political parties in Zambia have failed to engender intraparty democracy. Some positions in political parties are ever reserved for certain individuals and anyone who attempts to challenge the status quo is branded a traitor. Politicians always argue for the need to deepen the country's democracy, except they don't say this should start from within their own backyards.

The post of party vice president provided a fair share of the drama. It was fiercely contested by wealthy party members, some of whom flexed their financial muscle to garner the vote. The front runner was Austin Chewe, a retired army captain turned millionaire businessman. Others were Bwalya Chiti, a Lusaka lawyer and businessman who had risen through the party ranks, Elias Mpondela, another Lusaka businessman and Lupando Mwape, then party trustee and Vice President of the Republic.

The tribunal 'convicted' Chewe and subsequently expelled him from the party. Officially, he was expelled for corruption. But some MMD insiders claimed Chewe's expulsion was aimed at pre-empting what was circulated as his "planned ambush" on Mwanawasa by staging a surprise presidential bid. A former National Executive Committee member said the Mwanawasa camp "didn't want to leave anything to chance even though many of us knew that Mwanawasa would sail through overwhelmingly. If at all Chewe was interested in the presidency, he could certainly not have won it at the last minute. He simply didn't have the support to swing such a wonder."

The tribunal froze elections for vice president and the position remained vacant until 2011 when the MMD lost power.

Since the much-anticipated election of vice president was put off indefinitely, attention moved to the post of national secretary. It was a stunning election. Mwaanga, undoubtedly the most experienced politician in the MMD at the time, and Akashambatwa Mbikusita-Lewanika, a co-convenor of the Garden House Multi-party Conference, both lost to former Finance Minister and Chiengi legislator, Katele Kalumba. Mbikusita-Lewanika immediately announced his 'leave' from politics and went to his other beloved pursuit –

writing – where he relived his experience in a book *A Mulungushi Experience*. Mwaanga, ever the diplomat, remained useful to the party and was called upon to run Mwanawasa's re-election drive.

Kalumba was Mwanawasa's first Foreign Affairs Minister until he quit on 16 July 2002, the same day Parliament lifted Chiluba's immunity. Before the convention, he had reconciled with Mwanawasa and some party insiders claimed he had the President's blessing for the position. Mwanawasa was supposedly elated at his work as campaign manager for the Kankoyo Parliamentary by-election in the Copperbelt Province, which the party won. Mwanawasa's favourable attitude to Kalumba was nothing new. When he was under pressure not to appoint Kalumba to his first Cabinet for being implicated in the theft of K2 million from Parliament in 2001, Mwanawasa said, "Now the law we establish[ed] as MMD has cleared Honourable Katele Kalumba. As a man, I shouldn't prove him guilty. I have a lot of admiration for Honourable Katele Kalumba. I am happy that he was cleared by the Tribunal so that he can contribute in national development."

The convention was done. Mwanawasa did what is expected of every sensible leader – unite the victors and the vanquished. The party could not afford to go into a general election divided or else it would play into the hands of a surging opposition. Mwanawasa won re-election with 42% of the vote, up from 29% in 2001.

CHAPTER FIVE

THE CIRCLE AND THE SHOW

"In a society where wealth accumulates in the hands of a minority and power is concentrated in a few individuals, flattery flourishes as an art to benefit from those who wield power and authority. At times it is reciprocal. Those who flatter expect to get cash, grant of property, title, promotion, and safety in return of their praise. However, their agenda remains hidden so that they can manipulate the situation in their favour." – **Mubarak Ali, Pakistani historian, activist and scholar.**

BY DEFINITION OF function, the Office of the President remains as enshrined in the Constitution. But its character, reputation and modus operandi are continually shaped by the individual occupying it at a given time. Each incumbent brings their own experiences and values and how they conduct themselves while in that office defines its image.

One task Mwanawasa had upon assuming power was to give State House a new look. Previously, it had become a quintessence of numerous things - party affairs and a den of party cadres, a general extension of ministries, a dispenser of all manner of patronage, a handler of procurement, a fund-point for dubious projects and a rendezvous for all sorts of characters. The need to restore sanity and give the office a measure of dignity was not a matter of choice but necessity.

Less than a week in office, Mwanawasa banned individuals and organisations from seeking funding for projects from State House. In his heyday, Chiluba had millions of Kwacha allocated to him to dish out to whomsoever he wished. The Presidential Discretionary Fund – or the 'Slush Fund' as it was disreputably called – was taxpayers' money practically turned into one man's stipend. According to Chitala, Chiluba had used the fund to pay K5,000 each to his MPs for passing the controversial 1996 Constitution.

To have had State House dishing out taxpayers' money so recklessly and devoid of any accountability was cheapening the Presidency and making it a subject of unnecessary ridicule. It made State House appear as some huge cash dispenser. Chiluba defended it, but it remained nothing more than an act of institutionalised corruption. When Mwanawasa annulled the practice, some measure of sanity accrued to the office.

While he may have managed to change something about the image of State House, he failed to resist the notorious and potentially corrupt tendency of personally entertaining businessmen eager to cut deals with the country's topmost official. Businessmen dealing directly with the President want gratuitous advantages and privileges they would not ordinarily get if they went through the bureaucracy. They are well aware that the President's name is a huge asset through the remaining channels – if any. Thus, they are able to get a conclusive business deal over a cup of coffee or glass of whisky while others labour through the due process.

There are two examples of this. In April 2007, Mwanawasa told his supporters in Chipata, the Eastern provincial capital, that a banking tycoon had told him his bank was willing to lend the Food Reserve Agency K200 million to buy the harvest. In October, Mwanawasa said the same official had been to see him and disclosed that his bank was willing to finance the importation of oil to avert an impending fuel crisis in the country. According to Mwanawasa, the mandarins in the Ministry of Energy refused to entertain the bank official, preferring to call for tenders, in which case other interested businesses would have participated. Mwanawasa lambasted the bureaucrats for causing what he considered unnecessary delays when, in his words, someone had already offered to import the oil.

Oil procurement in Zambia has a chequered history. Under Chiluba, it was even handled by his economic advisor, Donald Chanda, who doubled as board chairperson of the defunct Zambia National Oil Company. He once circumvented tender procedures when he convened himself into a one-man tender committee and awarded an oil supply contract running into millions of dollars to the French oil firm Total, an indiscretion for which he later apologised before a parliamentary committee.

By chiding the energy officials, Mwanawasa was apparently encouraging the suspension of tender rules because a bank official had been to see him. Anti-corruption watchdogs criticised him although his lieutenants were quick to shield him. Government wished away the issue but not before the vocal opposition and civic groups demanded transparency. Mwanawasa perhaps realised how much he had underestimated the consequences of his action. He stepped aside and left his lieutenants to do the fire fighting. They caved in and revealed Finance Bank as the institution that had offered to import the oil. Rajan Mahtani, Mwanawasa's close friend, was the bank's chairperson.

Would any other bank official have managed to access the President and make a similar offer? Presidents don't negotiate loans. So why didn't Mahtani go to the Treasury?

Getting procedures wrong, making unguarded and costly statements, refusing to take responsibility and allowing his surrogates to massage his words were unfortunately sometimes part of Mwanawasa's style of administration. There were numerous instances where his juniors would claim, "The President was misunderstood." Had Zambians suddenly developed a legendary practice of misunderstanding their President's public statements? Or, as seems more likely, did Mwanawasa later realise that he had miscalculated the political repercussions of his statements but did not have the courage to own up publicly?

In *The State of Africa: A History of Fifty Years of Independence,* Martin Meredith narrates how Ghana's first President, Kwame Nkrumah, was duped by a Romanian businessman who convinced him to build a huge set of concrete silos to store cocoa, so that the price of cocoa could be controlled more effectively. But once built, the silos were condemned as unusable. In another case, one of Nkrumah's expatriate advisers, Robert Jackson, once walked into Nkrumah's office and found a European salesman peddling some farfetched scheme. Nkrumah had his pen in his hand ready to sign a contract for more than £1 million. 'Shall I just look it over, Mr. President?' suggested Jackson. He took the document away and that saved the exchequer £1 million.

I don't know if Mwanawasa was as easily persuaded as Nkrumah. But the conclusion from the preceding episode is that while it is the President's duty to ensure that government runs smoothly, this can be done without getting involved in operational issues like procurement. The President is there to ensure the smooth functioning of the entire administrative machinery rather than taking interest in matters that would better be left to relevant institutions and experts. How would the President discipline his subordinates if he is part of their mess?

The 'Big Man's' circle
Apart from Cabinet, Presidents have an inner circle of confidants who form a 'kitchen cabinet'. This circle regularly advises and influences key decisions. It can be a powerful clique, which - if left to its own whims and desires - can make the rest of the Executive largely redundant by simply whispering to the President what to say and do. Some ministers only see the President at official meetings or at public functions but this clique has unfettered access to him. Such access helps it to influence the President and thus it acquires a status higher than the rest of the appointees.

Chiluba had such a circle, comprising friends he came with from Ndola, those he worked with in the trade union movement and others that he drafted in along the way. One of the reasons Mwanawasa cited for his resignation in 1994 was that as Vice President he was ignored, and felt increasingly irrelevant as part of a Cabinet whose decision-making revolved around Chiluba's circle.

Prior to becoming President, Mwanawasa found himself in the midst of a group he had been politically detached from for seven years. The idea of running for President was not necessarily his. Neither did he own the campaign programme. He was merely asked to fit into what the party had designed. Therefore, he had very little leverage to manoeuvre and weave his own net of adherents. So when he formed his first Cabinet he engaged in a delicate

The Circle and the Show

juggling act by appeasing the old order while trying to create his own set. If he excluded the old guards, he would immediately be accused of discrimination and of being ungrateful for being installed in the position at the expense of other members. Mwanawasa also re-appointed some of the ministers who, under Chiluba, had acquired a public image of being disreputable.

However, some of his actions towards the old guard indicated that either their days in his team were numbered or he was not, in fact, interested in having them around. For instance, Chitalu Sampa had served as Chiluba's Defence Minister and was the party's national chairman. Mwanawasa appointed him as Deputy Minister in the same ministry. In reality, there was nothing wrong with this as the President makes executive decisions, except that having been a senior member of the party and government, Sampa expected more. Feeling belittled, he declined the appointment. Just as well he did. In his early days, Mwanawasa doubled as Defence Minister. It was unforeseeable how Sampa could work with him when he already felt demeaned. The fallout was imminent.

The lawyer friend

Mwanawasa brought with him to government some of his friends whom he appointed to key positions, forming his ring of strategists. He entrusted his ally George Kunda with the dual responsibility of Justice Minister and Attorney General. There were calls to have these two roles separated in the interest of independence. But Mwanawasa stayed put as his advisers argued that it was not the first time this was being done. They pointed to Gibson Chigaga and Fitzpatrick Chuula who held both positions simultaneously under Kaunda's government. Mwanawasa, however, changed position later when he relieved Kunda as Attorney General.

Kunda had been a part of Mwanawasa's defence team in the 2001 presidential petition in the Supreme Court. But Kunda became very unpopular, resulting in calls for his dismissal on the grounds that he was misleading Mwanawasa on many legal issues, especially constitutional reforms. He retained his position amid the storm, a sign that Mwanawasa retained confidence in him. He was the only minister Mwanawasa did not shuffle during his seven year presidency. Kunda later served as Vice President to Mwanawasa's successor.

Mr Cow Dung

In the Second Republic (1973-1990), Mwanawasa and Mundia Sikatana had acquired a reputation for taking up controversial cases other lawyers would not dare to for fear of incurring Kaunda's wrath. They studied law together at the University of Zambia; so they came a long way as friends. Mwanawasa's appointment of Sikatana as Agriculture Minister was widely viewed as a misplacement. But the veteran lawyer displayed enormous zeal in this portfolio, vowing to move Zambia from a food deficit to surplus. He argued for manure in place of chemical fertilizers. Some laughed off his theory and nicknamed him 'cow dung.' His tough talking added an interesting, if not comical, dimension to the heated debate on genetically-modified maize which Zambia rejected amid famine, earning the administration criticism from the West who had donated the grain.

Unflinchingly outspoken, Sikatana also threatened to lock up politicians who ransacked the Food Reserve Agency in unpaid loans running into millions of dollars. His anti-corruption rhetoric could have been personal conviction but it was also the master's language. By the time he left he did not say how many loans he recovered.

His courage ruffled some feathers. Within weeks of his appointment, he accused Chiluba's government of having siphoned off to the Bahamas US$90 million from the defunct Meridien BIAO Bank. There was no official government confirmation or denial. So Sikatana's statement stood. When Chiluba reacted, he was sure that "President Mwanawasa used his Minister of Agriculture" to attack him.

Sikatana's legal prowess was on display during the motion in Parliament to waive Chiluba's immunity. When Speaker Amusaa Mwanamwambwa told the movers of the motion that they had not complied with the provisions of circulating the motion twenty four hours before tabling it, the House became mired in a debate of procedure. Sikatana rose to the occasion and smashed the deadlock by quoting provisions of the Standing Orders that allowed the suspension of the twenty four hour procedure. The House then proceeded.

His stubbornness came in many shapes. According to Mulongoti, Sikatana wanted to contest as Member of Parliament in 2006 but Mwanawasa advised him against. "President Mwanawasa sent me as chairman for elections to tell him not to stand. He gave an assurance that he will nominate him again. When I told Mr Sikatana, he refused and told me he didn't want to be nominated. So he went ahead and applied to stand in Lusaka Central," Mulongoti recalled. "After some time, President Mwanawasa called me and when I got there, he showed me the list and laughed. There were thirteen applicants and Mr Sikatana came out number thirteen. The President said, 'look at your cousin. I already told him that I will nominate him but he still wants to stand.'"

After re-election, Mwanawasa made good of his word and re-nominated Sikatana and appointed him Foreign Affairs Minister, before dropping him on health grounds, although Sikatana denied being in poor health, pointing to his anti-Mugabe stance as the real reason for his dismissal. "President Mwanawasa had a soft spot for him," said Mulongoti, who also served as Sikatana's deputy at Foreign Affairs.

The reserved slot
Mwanawasa chose Lackson Mapushi as his Home Affairs Minister. Mapushi, a former school headmaster and a relative of Mwanawasa, was legislator for Keembe Constituency. The soft-spoken Mapushi died in a car accident in January 2003, just after a year in office. The slot remained vacant until Mwanawasa found his choice. The MMD adopted Ronnie Shikapwasha, Mwanawasa's relative, as candidate. A fighter pilot and reverend of Pentecostal faith, Shikapwasha served as commander of the Zambia Air Force from 1991 to 1997. He tried his luck at politics under the Heritage Party without success. He won Keembe and was immediately named Home Affairs Minister. That

the vacancy at Home Affairs waited for Shikapwasha, a Lenje and a relative for that matter, implied that the position was a preserve for family members – Mapushi and Shikapwasha being such.

Mwanawasa used the by-election campaign to give his people a piece of his mind.

I am still annoyed at the fact that my own people rejected me [in the 2001 elections after losing in his father's area in Chisamba]. Don't be mistaken that I will be pleased if the MMD lose this seat. Don't think that I will put Keembe on priority. Tongas, Ilas and Lenjes, we should not have any problems but my brother (Anderson Mazoka, a Tonga) is always insulting me. Brothers don't take each other to court [in reference to the 2001 presidential election petition]. Brothers embrace each other and I want to embrace him. I will be extremely sad if you don't give me Ronnie Shikapwasha.

Tribal and family bias haunted Mwanawasa throughout his stay in power. Most leaders are eternally guilty of this sin, but under Mwanawasa it appeared to have acquired elevated levels. There would be nothing wrong with his tribesmen and women and family members holding various public positions provided they were qualified. Gabriel Namulambe, then Minister of Sport, Youth and Child Development, and a Lamba by tribe like Mwanawasa, publicly made the point: "I belong to the family tree and I don't think it is wrong for President Mwanawasa to appoint people who belong to the tree who are competent to hold government positions."

When I interviewed Namulambe, he repeated the same line and claimed Mwanawasa led a "tribally balanced government at Cabinet, Deputy Minister and Permanent Secretary level."

Namulambe argued: "They were not all his relatives. They were tribesmates yes, but even if they were tribesmates, he didn't appoint riffraffs. They were all performers. So the statement that he presided over a family tree was not fair."

But was it a coincidence that Mwanawasa's tribesmates and relatives rose to various positions when he was in charge of making executive appointments?

Perhaps the worst was his appointment of his young brother, Harry, as deputy director of intelligence. By nature, the intelligence is a sensitive wing. Therefore, it is possible that even the head of intelligence could have felt intimidated to have the President's brother as one of his subordinates. He could have been viewed more as Mwanawasa's "eyes and ears" on the rest of the intelligence than a professional colleague in the service.

I do not recall any time when Mwanawasa publicly defended himself from accusations of nepotism. His handlers were seemingly helpless too, not knowing what defence to marshal on a matter that had become street talk and open for anyone to see and comment upon.

Mr HIPC

May 2003. The economy is in a mess. The treasury has bust the budget by over K600 million. The IMF has suspended aid and, together with its sister institution, the World Bank, is breathing heavily on government. There is no Finance Minister after Mwanawasa sacked Emmanuel Kasonde. Zambia was in danger of missing out on debt relief after years of austerity. Mwanawasa needed someone to realign and direct the economy. He picked Ng'andu Magande. His credentials were impeccable, having served in various local and international institutions.

Magande was a sympathiser of the opposition UPND and a friend of its leader, Anderson Mazoka. Much as his appointment was construed as Mwanawasa having a go at Mazoka, Magande's competence to oversee the economy could neither be doubted nor reduced to a settling of scores. Under his scrupulous approach, the economy made noticeable gains. Offensive as some might find it to partly attribute the success of economic policy to an individual, the role of competent leadership can never be underplayed. Magande was certainly a star technocrat in Mwanawasa's circle.

Some of his former Cabinet colleagues remember him as a tough fiscal disciplinarian. "I think he may have been one of the few ministers who could challenge Mwanawasa. He would tell him, 'Mr President, we can't do that because we don't have the money' and Mwanawasa would concede," said a former minister.

Fly to Paris, leave the mess
Mwanawasa's style of leadership was such that he would sometimes act quickly but at other times he would either act too late or not at all. In October 2005, the country experienced an acute shortage of fuel. The only refinery had been shut down. Long queues formed at service stations and industries cut back production, while experts warned the economy could slide into recession if the problem was not resolved.

Amid the crisis demanding urgent attention, Energy Minister George Mpombo flew to France to attend a conference. Incensed at Mpombo's poor judgment, Mwanawasa demoted him. This case was perhaps caution that it sometimes did not matter how close you thought you were to the nerve centre, you could still be detached.

A former district governor in the UNIP government, Mpombo served as provincial minister for Southern and Copperbelt provinces before making it to Cabinet under Energy. Upon re-election, Mwanawasa brought him closer as Defence Minister, which made him *de facto* number three. Excited with the media and famous for his explosive debates in Parliament where he unleashed grandiloquent speeches that had the House roaring with laughter, he always saw it as his duty to defend the master.

The fundraiser
Mwanawasa fired Vice President Kavindele after he was embroiled in an oil procurement scam with a South African firm, Trans Sahara Trading (TST). He had received K510, 000 from a TST official, Tony Teixeira, as a donation to the MMD. Mwanawasa also met Teixeira at Nkwazi House, the President's official residence. Teixeira told him about the money he gave Kavindele. According to Mwanawasa, the TST boss was blackmailing government by

The Circle and the Show

threatening to reveal to the media the donation made to the party if his firm was not allowed to supply fuel.

Mwanawasa was obviously discomfited that a party armed with hefty anti-corruption rhetoric was receiving kickbacks from corporations. In his dismissal letter to Kavindele on 28 May 2003, Mwanawasa said, "I was extremely embarrassed by the fact that neither myself nor the party secretariat were ever told of this money and to date only you know about the fact that it was given."

Justifying the donation, Kavindele told Mwanawasa that many other parties raised funds through donations from corporations and that if the MMD did not do the same, it risked becoming unpopular with party members who needed to be appeased with gifts. In reply, Mwanawasa said he would reject any gifts "offered with strings attached." He said the "favours" Kavindele had extended to TST to import fuel into Zambia were "completely unjustified and unauthorised." In April 2003 Mwanawasa had stopped TST from importing oil into Zambia, but it was apparently unknown to him that his deputy "gave authority for TST to bring in crude [oil]…without complying with agreements which TST signed with Indeni [Oil Refinery] and TAZAMA [Pipelines]."

Kavindele had his own version. Firstly, he acknowledged receiving K310,000 from the TST chairman, and not K510,000 as stated by Mwanawasa. Secondly, he said Mwanawasa had tasked him to fundraise for the party and the money from TST was part of the fundraising. Kavindele expressed surprise that Mwanawasa could "turn around" and accuse him of corruption. He also accused him of having allowed TST to import fuel into Zambia when he met Teixeira at Nkwazi House earlier in the year.

The story of oil procurement in Zambia has already been discussed.

I asked Kavindele about his fundraising activities. "We went to many business houses including TST. But I did not know those people (TST). Mwanawasa met them at his house. They had held several meetings including one where he lambasted Indeni [Oil Refinery] management for not giving TST the exact specifications. TST could not supply the oil because they didn't have the specifications. As for the donations, I handed over all the money to the party treasurer and two other officials who signed for its receipt. That is what saved me from being accused of stealing it."

The former Vice President said years later, after explaining to Mwanawasa how he handled the money, he complained about the public perception that he was fired because of his involvement with party donors and his alleged mishandling of the money. Mwanawasa then promised him that on return from Egypt, he would write a letter exonerating Kavindele from such accusations now that he understood the transaction. But as fate would have it, Mwanawasa died on that trip.

Kavindele's dismissal saw his relationship with Mwanawasa turn sour. He tried to stage a palace coup against his party boss but failed. He claimed it was unconstitutional for Mwanawasa to be acting party president. He said as the party vice-president, he should have taken over from Chiluba. In fact, Kavindele had had an opportunity to take over when Chiluba stepped down in 2002 but he had chosen not to for reasons discussed in Chapter Four. In addition, two months before his sacking, Kavindele, in a sworn affidavit in the High Court, had argued that the MMD's National Executive Committee constitutionally endorsed Mwanawasa after Chiluba stepped down.

When a party member, Mwaba Mushota, went to court to challenge Mwanawasa's leadership of the party, Kavindele appeared in court to defend his boss. So why did he want the party leadership now, I asked him? "Well, I was no longer Vice President of the Republic and felt I could take over," he said. Needless to say the opportunity had passed. Kavindele failed in his bid to overthrow Mwanawasa.

The adventurous deputy

Mwanawasa's actions when dealing with subordinates were by no means predictable. In October 2004 he was in New York for the United Nations General Assembly. In his absence, Vice President Nevers Mumba made a diplomatic gaffe by accusing "some individuals" in the Democratic Republic of Congo of backing the opposition in Zambia. Word reached Mwanawasa when his counterpart Joseph Kabila raised the issue with him. In the same month, Zambia was celebrating forty years of independence and government had planned a grand ceremony to mark the occasion. Whilst Mwanawasa was in New York, Mumba called a press conference where he talked at length about the 40th anniversary.

Mwanawasa took offence with both events. On arriving home, he did not wait for a briefing from his deputy. He publicly rebuked him at the airport: "I must say that the statement was extremely embarrassing to me since I am the Minister of Intelligence. Matters of this nature should be left to me to decide," he said of the Congo issue.

He also took issue with Mumba's press conference and claimed that never before in the history of Zambia had the Vice President addressed the nation. That was not true. While Chiluba was abroad, Godfrey Miyanda had addressed the nation and even had the unenviable task of announcing on state television the liquidation of Zambia Airways.

But such was the way Mwanawasa sometimes dealt with administrative matters. He sometimes had a crude and temperamental way of disparaging his officials. Even after that sting at the airport, Mwanawasa was not through yet.

At the airport receiving his boss, Mumba made another gaffe that only hastened his fate. Let loose by his aides and pounced on by the press, he said he did not regret his statement on the Democratic Republic of Congo. Mwanawasa squared the circle. He particularly took offence at Mumba's lack of regret on such a matter which he said was an act of defiance to authority.

Mumba tried to save face. He said he was not the first one to make the statement on the Democratic Republic Congo: the party's deputy national secretary, Richard Kachingwe, had done so before. It is true that Kachingwe had earlier made a similar statement in the Central Province town of Kabwe, but Mumba's case was certainly different as he was acting President at the time and could not afford to make a statement that not only put diplomatic relations on the line but also endangered national security. Mumba's handling of this issue exposed his naïvety with government affairs.

Earlier in the year, Mwanawasa had said of Mumba: "I have no intention of changing my Vice President because the few months we have been together, he has provided me with valuable assistance. God gave me a helper in the name of Dr Mumba. It will be a great sin to reject the help." The unstated fact was that Mwanawasa's confidence in Mumba was on condition that he did not do anything that threatened his boss's authority. Mumba made several blunders. But as long as he did not encroach on the master's space, he was tolerated.

Unknown to Mwanawasa, Mumba had started cultivating a support base within the MMD. He had already toured several constituencies in Lusaka until one day his tour was abruptly cancelled, after State House intervened. Journalists that were to cover Mumba's visit to one of the constituencies were simply told by his aides that he had to attend to other matters.

His decision to challenge for the party presidency was indicative of his ultimate target. Armed with flamboyance and fiery rhetoric, who could doubt his ability to sway? Had Mwanawasa's team not woken up and acted fast, they would have been stunned as Mumba would have been miles ahead in his presidential endeavours while Mwanawasa was still putting on his running shoes.

The loyalist par excellence

Mwanawasa's choice of his next deputy was the least expected. Lupando Mwape had served as Transport Minister under Chiluba and continued with Mwanawasa until he was sacked in 2003. He bounced back as Minister for Northern Province after which he was catapulted to be the country's number two. He was a loyal and less politically ambitious subordinate who gave Mwanawasa a break from the turbulent relationships he had had with his two previous deputies. Being the most unlikely of candidates for the position made him very loyal.

But his handling of government affairs could be quite clumsy. He was in charge of the country when Mwanawasa was hospitalised in London in April 2006. When the nation demanded answers about the President's condition,

Mwape gave a ridiculous response. He said the President was fine and was jogging in London. Where were the advisors and, much more importantly, other senior and experienced members of the government when such a lousy statement was made?

"Mwanawasa was very upset, he severely reprimanded Lupando Mwape. He told him 'I am not on holiday here'," disclosed Anderson Chibwa, who was then High Commissioner to London. "His illness was one of the most challenging issues I had to deal with as High Commissioner. Because of his high regard for transparency, he insisted that the Zambian public should be told the truth regarding his condition." However, in Lusaka the government played duck and dive. Only after sustained pressure did it announce that Mwanawasa had suffered a stroke.

In the 2006 election, Mwape was a victim of the rampaging opposition Patriotic Front who grabbed his Lukashya parliamentary seat in Kasama, Northern Province. Mwanawasa appointed him Ambassador to China.

The 'comeback kid'

In both Chiluba's and Mwanawasa's governments, Vernon Mwaanga was a pervasive feature. He was undoubtedly the most experienced politician in that crop; an interesting combination - journalist, diplomat, former intelligence boss, politician and election strategist (or 'election rigger', if you believe his accusers). He ran the MMD's 2001 and 2006 campaigns. But in between he differed with Mwanawasa when he was named among the beneficiaries of the looted intelligence account in London. He admitted receiving US$3,600 for supplying intelligence information, and not the US$360,000 Mwanawasa told Parliament.

Mwaanga charged: "Notwithstanding his pathological hatred for me as an individual, he swore to act without ill will towards anybody. But he is now misrepresenting me before Parliament."

Despite his differences with Mwanawasa, which were sometimes quite humiliating, Mwaanga remained at Mwanawasa's call. His dismissal in

2007 was thought to be the last and that even his reputation as an avowed political survivor would not give him a leap back into government. Mwaanga was sent to the Democratic Republic of Congo as special envoy. Congolese authorities had blocked trucks transporting copper concentrates into Zambia. From Kinshasa, Mwaanga proceeded to Katanga Province where he visited Moses Katumbi, governor of the province and a fugitive businessman who Zambia was pursuing at the time. Whilst there Mwaanga reportedly told the media that Zambia owed Katumbi US$7 million for maize he had supplied. In Lusaka, the version was that Katumbi owed Zambia the same amount. It was a deep running saga involving Parliament, the media and Mwaanga himself. Mwaanga said he was misquoted, but that didn't save him from being sacked.

In *The Long Sunset,* Mwaanga presents his version and attributes his dismissal to a "grand conspiracy" against him and "a blatant lie" told to Mwanawasa by an intelligence officer who accompanied him to the Democratic Republic of Congo. Mwaanga says the intelligence officer told Mwanawasa that Mwaanga met Katumbi for six hours at his hotel in Kinshasa, a report Mwaanga found puzzling. "Under a different set of circumstances, this issue would have been treated differently, but for the mistrust which had unhappily developed between Mwanawasa and myself," he says. In November 2007 Mwaanga announced his retirement from politics. But that was not the last of him.

Brought back: in name and in action

The Eastern Province was such a stronghold of UNIP that it even resisted the sweeping wind of change in 1991. The MMD only managed to win it after UNIP boycotted the 1996 election. But in 2001 the area fell back into opposition hands. As the 2006 election approached, it was clear that Copperbelt, Luapula and Northern provinces would be a tough call given Mwanawasa's fallout with Chiluba's supporters. The MMD desperately needed to tap into new areas with the support of influential figures. In Eastern Province, they identified Rupiah Banda, a former UNIP stalwart who had retired to his home district of Chipata. Banda campaigned for the MMD and won the province. After winning re-election, Mwanawasa invited Banda to be his deputy, a new entrant into the circle. Earlier in the year, I had met Banda at a function at the Kenneth Kaunda International Airport when he was a board member of the National Airports Corporation. Sporting a neatly pressed navy blue suit, he told me he had not worn it for two years as he spent most of his time at the farm in shorts. Little did he know that in six months' time, he would be Vice President and would be required to wear suits often.

Fearing for the master

Loyalty to a leader can sometimes make followers do strange things. Mwanawasa's circle were so eager to protect the throne that they sometimes acted in a manner that not only embarrassed government but also exposed their self-created state of insecurity. On more than one occasion, they screamed coup d'états. In a bid to draw public sympathy towards Mwanawasa and also paint black the opposition and disgruntled MMD members, they claimed "some people who looted the economy" had schemed to overthrow Mwanawasa. Zambia has seen four attempted coups – in 1980, 1988, 1990, and 1997 – but for Mwanawasa's cheerleaders the use of allegations of a coup attempt to discredit their opponents was a defective political strategy.

In 2002, the government had alarmed the nation unnecessarily over allegations of a coup attempt. A year later, it was Shikapwasha on the offensive: "The plunderers have gone to organise using the money they stole to remove Mr Mwanawasa from power. We know their plot. Their plan is organised on ethnic lines but is bound to fail. They have gone from country to country and Europe to source funding get the money they stole."

In 2005 it was Webby Chipili, deputy minister at State House, trying to divert attention from a fuel crisis facing the nation. Understandably, the government was under fire for its poor management of the petroleum subsector, but to use a fictional coup attempt as a red herring was unreasonable.

Throughout his first term, Mwanawasa remained politically insecure. His victory was in dispute and he viewed Chiluba's group with suspicion, convinced they were out to 'fix' him for 'betraying' them. But it is surprising that such a legalistic government that pledged to uphold the Rule of Law could allow 'coup plotters' to have a field day. Some government-sponsored NGOs slammed the hoax coup plotters. Governments may tolerate criticism but not subversion. Why would Mwanawasa's be an exception? His supporters were anxious to make him popular. But their tactics were sloppy and smacked of a regime keen to preserve itself amid a crisis of legitimacy.

CHAPTER SIX

BATTLES ACROSS THE DIVIDE

"I am no believer in the amalgamation of parties, nor do I consider it as either desirable or useful for the public; but only that, like religious differences, a difference in politics should never be permitted to enter into social intercourse or to disturb its friendships, its charities or justice." –
Thomas Jefferson (1743 -1826), 3rd President of the USA, 1801 - 1809.

MWANAWASA'S VICTORY IN the 2001 election was challenged in the Supreme Court. The opposition vowed not to recognise his leadership because they firmly believed he was fraudulently installed. United Party for National Development leader Anderson Mazoka declared,"We will never recognise Mwanawasa's illegitimate election and will pursue a multi-pronged legal campaign to have his victory nullified." On the other hand, Mwanawasa was determined to assert his authority and show his opponents that he was in charge until the courts decided otherwise.

These opposing positions ignited sparks that dominated much of Mwanawasa's first term. Although he had won round one of the battle against Chiluba elements in the party, he had yet another outside. He needed a more rational way of dealing with his opponents given their grievances. He repeatedly appealed to them to leave legal matters to the courts and invited them to work with him. But they spurned him, saying that would legitimise the very leadership they were challenging in court.

In the election aftermath, the opposition enjoyed a slim parliamentary majority. The MMD had won sixty nine seats, UPND forty nine, UNIP thirteen, FDD twelve, Heritage Party four, ZRP one, PF one and one independent. In total, the opposition commanded eighty one of the 150 elective seats. Adding the eight MPs nominated by the President to the MMD's sixty nine was still not sufficient to surpass the opposition. This was the first time since it came to power in 1991 that the MMD had lost its parliamentary majority. This posed a danger to the party as they would have difficulties passing legislation and other key reforms. The first hurdle the MMD faced was the election of the Speaker. The opposition had settled for Frederick Hapunda, former legislator for Siavonga and Deputy Chairperson of Committees in Parliament. Going by the numbers, the opposition was set to win the Speakership.

Mwaanga confesses engaging in "ingenious schemes" to convince some opposition parliamentarians to vote for the MMD candidate Amusaa Mwanamwambwa. Heritage Party legislators Gladys Nyirongo and Patrick Musonda, UPND's Sipula Kabanje and Independent Joseph Kasongo voted for Mwanamwambwa, thus helping the MMD to win the Speakership. This was the beginning of trouble for these opposition parliamentarians. With the exception of Kasongo who had no party allegiance, the other three were expelled from their parties. As a reward for their betrayal of the opposition, the MMD adopted them in subsequent by-elections and they returned to Parliament on the ruling party ticket.

The opposition were still annoyed at the manner they had lost the Presidency and now they had lost the Speakership owing to more underhand methods by the MMD. The rift between Mwanawasa and the opposition was widening.

In 2003 Mwanawasa took a route that angered his opponents even further. He enticed individual opposition MPs and appointed them as Cabinet and deputy ministers. Whether driven by a genuine desire for public service or mere personal ambition, those approached accepted. The opposition accused Mwanawasa of undermining parliamentary democracy. The MPs were only opposition by ticket but MMD in character and conduct. Not only did Mwanawasa's decision result in more strained relations between him and his opponents, but also created bad blood between the respective opposition MPs and their parties.

A day before Mwanawasa appointed opposition MPs, the High Court granted Heritage Party leader Godfrey Miyanda an injunction restraining Mwanawasa from making the appointments. But Mwanawasa blasted High

Court judge Anthony Nyangulu for granting the injunction as the President cannot be sued in his private or official capacity. In addition, the State Proceedings Act insulates the State from injunctions. Ideally, the judge was better off keeping quiet after that gaffe, but he made a strange apology, saying he was unwell when granting the injunction. How many other decisions he might have made in a similar state is a fair question to ask.

Mwanawasa raised his numbers in Parliament by undermining the opposition and by creating chaos in their camp. Even in his own party, there was discontent over his decision to reward opposition members at the expense of his own, some of whom felt they had sacrificed a lot to help him win the presidency and wondered why he had chosen to fish from outside the pond.

Some of Mwanawasa's supporters mockingly told the opposition that the Constitution stated that 'the President shall appoint ministers from among Members of Parliament.' Therefore, they argued, Mwanawasa had done nothing illegal. There are times when the law is quoted to aid expediency and this was one of them. In any case, no one had accused Mwanawasa of acting illegally. The issue was how he was trying to decimate the opposition using what he himself interpreted as good intentions.

Opposition parties reacted angrily by expelling the MPs appointed to ministerial posts. The UPND expelled its secretary general and Solwezi Central MP Benny Tetamashimba, deputy secretary general and Nangoma MP Kennedy Shepande, and Kaoma Central MP Austin Liato. What turned out to be even more agonising for the UPND was that they lost all the seats in the subsequent by-elections to their former MPs who stood on the MMD ticket. The FDD expelled Lusaka Central MP Dipak Patel, Chawama MP Geoffrey Samukonga, Matero MP Chance Kabaghe and Mandevu MP Patricia Nawa. But the FDD quartet succeeded in hanging onto their seats via prolonged court processes until Parliament was dissolved in readiness for the 2006 election.

Mwanawasa had repeatedly said he wanted to work with the opposition. His first invitation was in his inaugural speech in which he said, "To my colleagues who aspired for this position, I salute you and respect you for the good fight we had. Now the nation needs your positive contribution because we all want a better life for our people..."

Was he genuine or was he just trying to deal with the insecurities of a minority leader?

The opposition were in no mood to work with him. Mwanawasa should have understood that given the circumstances under which he came to power, the opposition would have no reason to change their view that he was an illegitimate leader with whom they would not cooperate. So the forced unity that Mwanawasa pursued was neither necessary nor desirable in the eyes of the opposition.

Clearly, it was not unity Mwanawasa was seeking. It was about political survival through weakening the opposition, using supposedly good intentions. It is worth noting that after being re-elected and emerging with considerable strength at presidential and parliamentary level, he did not need the opposition and thus was not as desperate to work with them as he had been in his first term. That explained his true intentions earlier.

Mwanawasa and his opponents were engaged in explosive political battles. They accused him of incompetence and implacably criticised his leadership, claiming they could do better. He responded to every brickbat hurled at him. This was in stark contrast to Chiluba who would take time to respond to attacks or not at all. It is my considered view that he or indeed his aides would have done better to follow Chiluba's example in this instance as his responses not only ignited more sparks but gave courage to his opponents to taunt him even further, knowing he would respond. His responses were an unconscious admission that they had succeeded in keeping him on his toes.

Engaging the 'cheated'

Mwanawasa's Presidency coincided with the return of a competent opposition. Since UNIP boycotted the 1996 election, there was virtually no opposition to the MMD. The formation of the UPND in 1998 was the beginning of a plausible check to the MMD. With a fine collection of intellectuals and an array of alternative policies, the party arguably gave the MMD a good run.

While Mwanawasa and Mazoka may not have had anything personal against each other, their relations, as political opponents, were not expected to be all rosy, especially as Mazoka believed he was a victim of election fraud which had handed Mwanawasa the victory. There were attempts by the two at working together. But their meeting in 2002 at Mark Chona's house failed to yield any result. Chona served as Kaunda's aide. I contacted him to shed light on this meeting, but he declined.

Interestingly, in May 2003, Benny Tetamashimba made the startling claim that Mazoka had sent him to Mwanawasa to negotiate the Vice-Presidency on his behalf. It's difficult to make sense of that claim. Mazoka had a face-to-face meeting with Mwanawasa at Chona's house a year earlier. So, if indeed Mazoka had revised his position and was now interested in working with Mwanawasa, he would have simply contacted Mwanawasa, who was deeply insecure and desperate to work with the opposition. It is highly unlikely he would have spurned a partnership with Mazoka, a man reputed to have won the election. Given the foregoing, it is doubtful that, although Tetamashimba was once one of Mazoka's confidants, he would have been the emissary to deliver the Vice-Presidency. Additionally, it would have been hypocritical of Mazoka to denounce Mwanawasa in public whilst canvassing for a partnership in private. If Tetamashimba was to be believed, then one would have to question Mazoka's sincerity.

Having fallen out with Chiluba, Mwanawasa remained suspicious of people who dealt with his predecessor. Any moves by his rivals to embrace Chiluba added to his insecurity. Mazoka attempted to lure Chiluba into testifying for him in the presidential petition. In March 2002 Chiluba visited Mazoka at his residence. When it leaked, Mazoka blundered by denying he met Chiluba. But he later u-turned and admitted that Chiluba had indeed visited. This was what became known as 'the meeting under a tree.'

Later in September of the same year, it emerged that there had been meetings between UPND and Chiluba to get him to testify for the petitioners. Given the underhand methods the MMD employed to win the election, as was revealed in the Supreme Court, the prospect of having Chiluba as a star witness must have excited the UPND.

But as it turned out, Mazoka probably didn't know the people he was dealing with. He was betrayed; the minutes of the planning meeting were leaked to Mwanawasa. He was furious and accused Mazoka of collaborating with plunderers to remove him from power. In his letter to Mazoka, Mwanawasa accused him of "an insatiable desire to get to State House at all costs" and of pursuing "fraudulent means to secure court indemnity against prosecution for people suspected to have plundered national resources." As far as Mwanawasa was concerned, the meetings between UPND and Chiluba were aimed at removing him from power and eventually letting Chiluba go scot-free.

Chiluba was under fire from MMD members who demanded he leave the party to join UPND. But he was unmoved, arguing that everyone in Zambia was free to meet him including opposition members. "If MMD cadres find it difficult to visit me, other people will find it easy to visit me," Chiluba said, nonchalantly. Given the hostile relationship between Chiluba and Mwanawasa, it was obvious that Mwanawasa and his supporters would respond the way they did to reports of Chiluba scheming with the opposition.

For his part, Mazoka had argued in his response to Mwanawasa that his legal team was at liberty to "identify and assess the suitability and credibility of the available witnesses and their evidence." Broadly interpreted, Mazoka was prepared to meet anyone who would help him win the presidential petition. It was in the public domain that Mwanawasa's election was soiled with corruption and the petition in the Supreme Court was aimed at proving that. However, the petition also exposed Mazoka's desperation to win his case if he was even prepared to be in cahoots with people of questionable repute.

Some of the people Mazoka met as Chiluba's agents posed as *bonafide* civil society leaders, but were in fact known to be nothing less than hired political mercenaries eager to engage in deceptive schemes that would endear them to the highest bidder. They were the same people Chiluba had hired outside MMD to support his third term bid after, ironically, they had initially denounced it. But since money was dangled in front of their faces, they had no trouble revising their conscience. In addition to UPND officials personally meeting Chiluba, these fake political consultants were the people Mazoka was also relying on to get Chiluba to be the star witness.

Mazoka and UPND were under the erroneous impression that Chiluba's much sought after testimony would be so damaging that it would automatically lead to the annulment of Mwanawasa's election. There was no such guarantee, unfortunately. In the event that Chiluba took to the stand to admit he rigged the election in Mwanawasa's favour, he ran the risk of being indicted for a criminal act. These talks, however, did not yield anything.

The political damage to Mazoka arising from this was immense, although he seemed unaware of it. The overtures he made to Chiluba undermined his consistency. On the one hand, Mazoka and UPND were on record denouncing Chiluba as a criminal; on the other, they were attempting to get him to back their cause. If Chiluba was a criminal, how clean would his testimony be, if they even cared, anyway? Suppose the deal had gone through and Chiluba testified, what was in it for him? Were Mazoka and UPND going to recant their earlier position that Chiluba was a criminal? Or would they simply have disowned the deal and left Chiluba guessing in the cold?

Shortly after the press conference he had called at his residence to deny Mwanawasa's charges of colluding with Chiluba, I interviewed Mazoka on the matter and his response was, "If he (Mwanawasa) has evidence that I am interfering with the course of justice, let him go to court." This was something Mazoka said in a relaxed, gentlemanly tone while sipping his Coca-Cola. However, when I asked him how he thought his supporters and the nation at large would perceive him given reports that he was meeting people of questionable repute in his desire to win the presidential petition, he winced, became upset and asked me what I was up to. I ended the interview. But his response spoke volumes about just how touchy that issue was.

Mwanawasa's fallout with Chiluba brought about scenarios that were not envisaged. If Mwanawasa had acted according to Chiluba's script by being his puppet, the idea of Chiluba being courted to testify for the opposition would not have arisen. Even the Chiluba loyalists who testified against Mwanawasa would not have been so brazen in their accounts of what they did to win the election.

Although politics is a popularity contest and a struggle of egos, Mwanawasa and Mazoka's differences were not feudal.

Mazoka, a US-trained mechanical engineer, was one of Zambia's high-flying corporate elites who rose through the ranks in the parastatal sector and ended up as Anglo American CEO for Central Africa, sitting on forty two boards and chairing eighteen of them. He founded the UPND after retiring from Anglo in 1998. Mwanawasa honoured him as a national leader following his death on 24 May 2006. One obituary described him as "the president Zambia never had."

Mazoka was replaced by Hakainde Hichilema, a sharp-suited tycoon who until then was not publicly known to have had an interest in politics; he was known more as a boardroom guru and a facilitator of multibillion dollar business deals. However, he had been a member of the UPND and was one of its financiers. Mwanawasa attempted to work with Hichilema just as he came onto the scene. This was a strategic move. Elections were due in four months and if he could get Hichilema into an alliance, this would boost his fortunes at the general election. But the opposition had other plans as Hichilema discovered. An opposition alliance had already been hatched comprising the UPND, FDD and UNIP. How could a newcomer, therefore, drag the party to the other side of the river?

The bungled assignment

Godfrey Miyanda was another of Mwanawasa's opponents. A retired army officer, he was not the antagonistic type. A keen reader of the law, he on several occasions challenged the legality of some government actions. Shortly before the 2006 election he raised a storm that got the government and lawyers running. He argued that the constitution didn't allow the President to set the election date even though that had been the practice based on an established tradition. The Law Association of Zambia (LAZ) swung into action and sought the interpretation of the law in the courts. They also placed an injunction to stop the President from setting the poll date. Getting mired in legal hitches ahead of a crucial election was the last thing Mwanawasa was prepared to face. He acted swiftly, rushing through Parliament a new Electoral Act that specifically provided for the President to set the date in consultation with the Electoral Commission.

Although the court dismissed the injunction, it allowed LAZ to challenge the legality of the president setting the date. But that would be an academic exercise as Mwanawasa had already dissolved Parliament and set the poll date. Such were Miyanda's legal exploits. In the presidential petition, he was his own 'lawyer'.

Preferring to stay out of the daily political chatter, he chose to issue well researched policy statements. While Miyanda and Mwanawasa had differences regarding governance, these differences did not lead to personal attacks.

In 2006 the MMD attempted to lure Miyanda back to their camp but the emissary, one of the aides at State House, bungled the assignment, earning him the sack. Miyanda also publicly disclosed that Mwanawasa had sent his nephew Jonas Shakafuswa to invite him to re-join the party.

Dealing with the 'King Cobra'

The rivalry between Mwanawasa and Sata was historical. They fell out when they served in Chiluba's government in the 1990s. Once, when Chiluba was abroad and Mwanawasa was acting President, a report reached Mwanawasa about Sata's alleged corruption. He recommended Sata's prosecution, but when Chiluba returned, he only wrote a letter asking Sata to exculpate himself. In a letter to Mwanawasa dated 24 June 1994, Sata went on the offensive and launched a stinging attack on him, alleging he was "very unfit" to hold the second highest position in the land. Chiluba, in a letter dated 26 June 1994, in turn censured Sata for attacking Mwanawasa and said his action amounted to a lack of respect for authority.

Mwanawasa's resignation in 1994 provided a ceasefire. But his return reignited the old rivalry. At the selection of a presidential candidate for the MMD, Sata reckoned it was dividend time. He had worked hard to denounce those that opposed Chiluba's third-term bid, thinking the prize would eventually be his if and when Chiluba bowed out. But he was by far the biggest loser and the heaviest casualty of Chiluba's scheming. It was quite a rude awakening that the candidacy landed on Mwanawasa. That Sata was denied the candidacy was in itself a tragedy for him, but that it went to his chief antagonist was an additional slap in the face.

Chiluba was alive to the differences between Mwanawasa and Sata and must therefore have anticipated the fallout. But at that stage, Chiluba was more prepared to have his way than retain any sentimental feelings for one of his loyalists, no matter how hard they had worked for him. In the very unlikely event that Sata had masked his contempt for Mwanawasa and pretended to accept his candidature, the differences would be too obvious even to the most disinclined follower of politics.

When he was given the candidacy, Mwanawasa was not anywhere near the internal politics of the MMD. But that still did not spare him from Sata's bashing. Sata's resignation letter dated 24 September 2001 said it all. He bluntly told Chiluba that he would not campaign for Mwanawasa and that, if elected, Mwanawasa would be to Zambia what Abel Muzorewa and Ian Smith were to Zimbabwe. This comparison could only have come from a sworn enemy. The floodgates of personal tussles were flung open once again.

Four months into Mwanawasa's Presidency, Sata was arrested and prosecuted for the theft of two motor vehicles. 'Theft of motor vehicle' is a controversial offence in Zambia which has notoriously been used to fight political battles. Its notoriety lies in the fact that it's a non-bailable offence. It has its roots in fighting love battles, as it was one law Chiluba is said to have specifically created to 'fix' a man he suspected of flirting with his wife. The man was jailed on that charge. For Sata, his arrest had nothing to do with any crime but was an act of vengeance by Mwanawasa whom he accused of using

State power to fight opponents. Sata spent over forty days in prison but had the last laugh when the court acquitted him with a ruling that he had handed over the vehicles when he left government. "He failed to break me," he mocked Mwanawasa, seemingly feeling satisfied that he had won the round.

Three years on, in 2005, Mwanawasa ordered Sata's arrest for inciting miners at Konkola Copper Mines to plant explosives in the mine as part of their strike action. This case pended in the courts for years. In the interim, Sata would even have the luxury to dare the State on why he was not being prosecuted.

At a meeting of presidential candidates at the Electoral Commission a month before the 2006 polls, their rivalry became very public when they engaged in a bitter exchange of words outside the offices. Their differences – both political and personal – were historically well documented but that incident alone was very embarrassing for their image, even more so for old men seeking to lead a nation.

Sata's links with Taiwan prior to the election brought him in close collision with Mwanawasa. Sata received funding from Taiwan. (As a matter of fact, several opposition parties in Africa have financially exploited Taiwan with a promise that they would recognise it once they formed government. In its attempt to outdo Beijing, Taipei has parted with some handsome cash). After the election, Sata continued seeking funding from Taiwan and one of his money-seeking letters to the Taiwanese Ambassador in Malawi was published in the press.

As is well known, China is Zambia's esteemed partner. So Sata's support for Taiwan – which China considers to be its province – and his contemptuous attitude towards the Chinese strained relations between Zambia and China. Sata had promised woe to exploitative investors, a synonym for the Chinese. There was a joke that when Sata was leading the presidential race, casual workers at Chinese-owned firms were given long-term contracts. China, meanwhile, had announced it would cut diplomatic ties with Zambia if Sata won. Given the massive investment by China in Zambia, this worried government, which found it necessary to apologise to Beijing over Sata's conduct.

As results of the election poured in, Sata was in the lead and he commenced preparations for his inauguration, instructing Cabinet Office to include the Taiwanese Ambassador to Malawi on the guest list. When the rural vote came in, the scales changed; Mwanawasa won the election by 42% against Sata's 29%. Sata fumed and accused Mwanawasa of stealing the vote; his supporters went on the streets but, to his credit, Sata appealed for calm and further chaos was averted.

Post-election, Sata and his Patriotic Front emerged as the main opposition. Powered by his increased strength in Parliament and local councils, he was yet again to be a constant thorn in Mwanawasa's flesh. He vowed to make Mwanawasa's life difficult "both inside and outside Parliament" and announced that they would share government; he would run the local government while Mwanawasa would superintend central government. Fresh from being confirmed for a second term, Mwanawasa did not mince his words and told Sata not to "push his luck too far because I will sort him out."

In December 2006 Sata was arrested and charged with false declaration of assets. But the court threw out the case.

Sata flew to Malawi in March 2007 for what he said was a business meeting. On arrival in Blantyre, authorities deported him to Zambia. Sata accused Lusaka of being behind his deportation, claiming they told their Malawian counterparts that he was there to help former president Bakili Muluzi campaign following his reported political comeback. As stated earlier, Muluzi anointed Bingu Wa Mutharika as his successor, but it was one of those plans that went awfully wrong. Given the bad blood between Muluzi and Mutharika, even if what Zambia allegedly told Malawi was a lie, authorities there could not sit idle.

In November 2007 government temporarily withdrew Sata's passport to probe how he acquired it. Sata was on his way to the United States but claimed he lost his passport in London. He flew back to Lusaka on a traveller's document issued by the Zambian High Commission in London, obtained another passport and flew out again. The government said Sata did not follow procedure in obtaining the new passport. But they failed to state whether the Passport Office followed procedure in issuing Sata the new passport or whether the High Commission in London acted correctly before facilitating his travel back home. It was therefore quite illogical for the government to wonder if Sata acquired the passport legitimately when the Passport Office is a government department.

Was it by coincidence that the State did not succeed in any of these cases against Sata? The outcome, and the State's reluctance to pursue the cases, further lent credence to the view that it was merely using such arrests to silence Sata. Government also occasionally used Sata's former confidants and some State-sponsored 'NGOs' to dig up some 'dirty files' from the past to discredit him. In 1992, when he was Local Government Minister, Sata was probed, though not prosecuted, by the Anti-Corruption Commission over K1.2 million of public money which he was accused of putting into his personal bank account. It was such cases government would occasionally 'resurrect' in their bid to discredit Sata.

All these schemes that were used to bully Sata into submission certainly did not work. It is true that Mwanawasa was perennially irritated with Sata, but he was far from matching his abrasive style of politics. Mwanawasa actually engaged Sata in his comfort zone where Sata enjoyed being the hero. Mwanawasa would have been better off ignoring his stern critic. These scuffles only shoved Sata into the limelight and made him appear persecuted, even though some of his acts could not go unchecked legally or politically. But being the legalist he was, and also to prove that he was capable of taking on Sata, Mwanawasa did not miss a chance to demonstrate his capacity to fight back, regardless of whether it might be interpreted as a political vendetta.

The relationship between Mwanawasa and Sata was most eventful for its controversy. But in a dramatic turn of events, they are said to have reconciled before Mwanawasa's death. In April 2008 Sata suffered a heart attack. Within two hours, Mwanawasa had ordered his evacuation to South Africa. It was such a quick response that even without his passport – which Zambian authorities had seized months earlier – Sata was allowed entry into South Africa. Although there is no actual policy on who deserves treatment abroad, it is normally a preserve of the privileged and chosen few. That Mwanawasa extended this gesture to Sata earned him accolades of statesmanship, laying aside their differences at a critical hour.

After treatment, Sata returned home changed in at least three ways. Firstly, he said his health was much better. Secondly, following doctors' recommendation he had quit his chain-smoking habit after over forty years. Thirdly, he had adopted a new brand of politics – well, at least towards Mwanawasa.

Two days after arriving from South Africa, Sata, for the first time in seven years, entered State House "to say thank you" to Mwanawasa for facilitating his treatment. Mwanawasa spoke first: "Today [14 May 2008] is one of the important days of my administration. It is unfortunate that it must take a serious illness for all of us to realise just how much we need each other."

Sounding unusually respectful of Mwanawasa, Sata took his turn: "I am entitled [to treatment abroad]. Everybody is entitled but somebody has to make a decision at the right time. Your Excellency, I am very, very grateful." The two leaders later had an unprecedented ninety minutes private meeting where, it emerged, they had agreed to put the past behind them and work for the national good.

Sata then went on to describe the secret nature of their talks: "It will only be me who will know what has been discussed with President Mwanawasa. Not even Guy Scott [his deputy] will know. As colleagues, we must keep confidence of each other," Sata said of his newly found political accord. He resolved not to publicly criticise Mwanawasa but would instead talk directly to him – what a huge departure from what had been the norm.

There were some interesting reactions to the so-called reconciliation. Writing in his weekly column, political scientist Neo Simutanyi, stated that, "Many are sceptical about the reconciliation between Sata and Mwanawasa and see it as designed to serve Sata's personal agenda. Why should his expression of personal gratitude to Mwanawasa for saving his life result in such a massive policy shift?" He noted, though, that both leaders had "scored political capital from the gesture to work together."

In its editorial, *The Post* newspaper said, "We hope this reconciliation does not lead to political insulation, complacency and unchecked use of political power and indeed political degeneracy and decay. Reconciliation between leading politicians of the moment is a political phenomenon without inherent virtues." Others accused Sata of compromising the role of the opposition by choosing not to criticise Mwanawasa publicly. In turn Sata accused his critics of being jittery.

Sata took his party by surprise and it was a relief for those who were yearning for a change of his type of politics.

But history is not just made of what happens; it also consists of events that never were. Zambians never saw the real test of that reconciliation. Mwanawasa left the country a month later, never to return alive. It would have been worth observing how Sata's militant supporters would relate to the ruling party, with which they often clashed, or even how Sata would have in reality turned away from his grating political attitude.

On the basis of his meeting with Mwanawasa, Sata later started making startling claims. When Mwanawasa died, Sata claimed he had shared with him his plans for the country. Even more interesting was the claim that Mwanawasa had shared with him names of corrupt ministers he intended to fire. I did establish from some former insiders that Mwanawasa intended to reshuffle his Cabinet on his return from Egypt. But they expressed doubt that he would have shared that with Sata. "Maybe, but I doubt," a former aide said. "He was very discreet with how he dealt with such matters."

"If – and this is a big if – President Mwanawasa had gone so far as to share such inner details of his pending executive decisions, then we can only say he must have really been overwhelmed at the change in their relationship," a former minister added.

When Mwanawasa lay ill in a Paris hospital, Sata attempted to travel there. "I want to go and see my friend," he said, before government turned down his request. Contrast this with two years earlier when Mwanawasa was hospitalised in London; Sata caused a stir, camping at the Vice President's office demanding to discuss the matter and also petitioned the Chief Justice to appoint a panel of doctors to ascertain Mwanawasa's fitness to rule the country.

CHAPTER SEVEN

TRYING AND TESTING THE LAW

"The only conduct that merits the drastic remedy of impeachment is that which subverts our system of government or renders the president unfit or unable to govern." – **Charles Ruff (1939 - 2000), American lawyer.**

ON 28 MAY 2003, Mwanawasa dismissed Enoch Kavindele as Vice President and replaced him with Nevers Mumba. Mumba had lost the 2001 presidential election. His appointment carried with it a nomination as Member of Parliament. However, Article 68 (3) of the constitution stated that: "A person may not be appointed as a nominated member if he was a candidate for election in the last preceding general election or in any subsequent by-election."

Based on that, the opposition made a case against Mwanawasa and planned to impeach him. They alleged that in terms of Article 37 (1) and (2), Mwanawasa deserved impeachment for "violating the Constitution and for gross misconduct." But Mwanawasa, himself a lawyer of immense standing, insisted that he had "consulted widely before making the appointment" and that in his view, his decision was justified.

Mumba was appointed when Parliament was on recess. In the interim, the opposition galvanised themselves into the Inter-parliamentary Caucus on the Defence of the Constitution and Good Governance (ICDCGG) and planned an impeachment once the Legislature reconvened. They originated a petition and collected 57 signatures from MPs. Among those that signed the petition were five MMD parliamentarians. Kavindele was one of them and he laid 32 documents in Parliament accusing Mwanawasa of pocketing US$60,000 of donated party funds. I asked Kavindele why he did that. Was he bitter for being fired? "Not at all," he argued, "I just thought Mr Mwanawasa had become what we didn't think he would. To him, the term 'corruption' was a term he used to threaten people he thought threatened his power base."

Others were Luapula MP Peter Machungwa, Chembe MP Dalton Sokontwe, Kalulushi MP Chitalu Sampa and Chiengi MP Katele Kalumba – all Chiluba loyalists in very bad books with Mwanawasa. While they were entitled to participate in testing the law, their aim was to use the opportunity to hit back at Mwanawasa.

Edith Nawakwi, then vice president of the FDD, challenged the constitutionality of Mumba's appointment in the High Court. She also applied for an injunction to block Mumba from being sworn in as MP. However, the court dismissed the application for an injunction saying it would not be in the public interest. It further said that under the State Proceedings Act, Mumba enjoyed immunity from prosecution.

The resumption of Parliament was eagerly expected as the country waited to see how the action initiated by the opposition would pan out. Mumba was sworn in amid opposition protests. The ICDCGG argued that he was a 'stranger' in the House and a product of an illegal decision. They boycotted Parliament for eight days.

Two versus one

The conference room at Pamodzi Hotel was packed. Opposition leaders Anderson Mazoka, Christon Tembo and Michael Sata graced the high table. Mazoka and Tembo, leaders of UPND and FDD respectively, supported the boycott. But Sata opposed it and instead urged the parliamentarians to fight from within the House. He told them they were missing "a golden opportunity" by boycotting. Armed with history, he pointed to a case in the UNIP era where Kaunda made a similar appointment of Justin Chimba who had lost an election but Parliament revoked the appointment. Mazoka appeared astonished as he turned to listen to Sata. Tembo sat still, facing down. But Sata's voice was insignificant as UPND and FDD with the bulk of MPs eventually dictated proceedings. "*Lwenu ulo, ine nimyeba* (It's up to you, I have done my part)," Sata remarked as he meandered through the crowd at the end of the joint opposition press conference.

Trying and Testing the Law

On Tuesday 12 August 2003 the impeachment motion was finally tabled in Parliament. UPND chief whip Crispin Sibetta, an eloquent parliamentary veteran who first set foot in the Legislature in the Second Republic, spiritedly moved the motion. In their Notice of Motion, the opposition advanced twenty five grounds for the President's impeachment. The Executive bench countered, with Justice Minister George Kunda saying the motion was set "merely to scandalise the President based on false, irrelevant and unsubstantiated and flimsy allegations" as it did not meet the criteria in Article 37.

After an intense two day debate, the matter was put to a vote. The MMD, with support from some opposition MPs co-opted into the Executive, got ninety two votes against the opposition's fifty seven. That result was expected. The opposition, more than anyone else, should have known better the futility of their actions. Their plan was doomed to fail from conception.

Firstly, the opposition knew they did not have sufficient numbers to win such a crucial vote. Passing it needed a two-thirds majority which translated into 106 MPs. They knew they were nowhere near that number. Yet they proceeded. Their bet on secret voting, in which they had hoped some more potentially disgruntled MMD MPs would vote with them, was a stretched fantasy. Voting was by open division. Besides, what was decisive was having a good case and not necessarily the mode of voting.

Secondly, it would seem the opposition were in so much of a hurry that they did not stop to analyse their strategy. Although Mwanawasa claimed to have "consulted widely", there was no doubt that he had violated the law by his nomination of Mumba, who was a losing candidate in the immediate past election. In fact, when the impeachment motion came up in Parliament, MMD MPs did not bother to debate that aspect, well aware of the inconvenient truth. Instead, they took advantage of the opposition's disorganisation to wholly dismiss the indictment as political sour grapes. Instead of dealing with Mumba's issue, which was their initial grievance, the opposition tried to include many others, which they knew would not stick in a motion of impeachment.

For instance, painful as it was to the opposition, there was no law that prevented Mwanawasa from appointing opposition MPs to the Executive. Yet the opposition saw it fit to include that issue on the motion of impeachment. Impeachments of most heads of states around the world have been based on specific, solid cases, and not on the hefty and excessively ambitious twenty five presented by Zambia's opposition. The whole plan was ill-conceived and badly executed.

The opposition's desperation could not have been better illustrated by their duplication of effort. They took Mumba's case to court and also raised it before Parliament. It is parliamentary practice not to discuss matters that are before the courts – at least that principle has been applied in some cases before. But Mumba's case somehow 'sneaked in'. Whether that was a conscious decision or not is a matter legal researchers can consider and debate upon. Suffice to say it was a huge political experiment. Suppose the opposition had successfully impeached Mwanawasa and later the courts ruled in his favour over the Mumba case, what would have happened? Parliament and the Judiciary would have crossed swords – a constitutional crisis triggered by a frenzied lust for power.

The opposition formulated what they called a "10-point action plan" which they openly said was aimed at making the country ungovernable and forcing Mwanawasa out of power. Could they have been more irresponsible? There is no doubt that Mwanawasa committed several errors of omission and commission. However, whether he deserved impeachment is a matter of grave doubt. But if he did, his accusers would have to point to credible charges, and not to the wild political tantrums they took to Parliament.

Charles Ruff, a former White House counsel who defended Bill Clinton during his fight against impeachment following his sex scandal with Monica Lewinsky, said something worth pondering upon in this context: "The only conduct that merits the drastic remedy of impeachment is that which subverts our system of government or renders the President unfit or unable to govern." If Ruff's supposition is to be used as a yardstick, we may well ask, did Mwanawasa reach the level described by Ruff?

Trying and Testing the Law

In countries that have impeached presidents or disagreed with the regimes on their approach to governance, the people normally first revolt and Parliament or any other institutions are merely asked to endorse the people's demands. Such was the case, for instance, in the Philippines when citizens marched on the capital Manila in 2000, calling for the impeachment of their corrupt leader, Joseph Estrada. He was impeached, arrested, tried and convicted.

If Zambians were convinced Mwanawasa deserved impeachment, it would be after they had found a watertight case against him, rather than relying on the opposition's defective charge sheet, which was, in fact, nothing but a tool to settle scores.

When the government said the impeachment attempt was aimed at embarrassing the President and the country before the international community, the opposition shamelessly agreed. If an onerous task like managing public affairs could be reduced to who embarrasses whom, then it shows how simplistic the people we call 'our leaders' can sometimes be.

The opposition have a critical role to play in a democracy as they provide checks and balances to the party in power. As competitors for power and as the so-called 'government in waiting', they have views and ideas on what the country needs and how it should be governed. In Zambia's nascent democracy, the opposition have been vibrant in fulfilling their basic role in checking government. They have advocated for policies and programmes in the interest of the people. They have also proposed solutions to the many challenges facing the country. That is commendable. But it is also true that there have been times when their zeal has been grossly misplaced and their impeachment bid stands out in that respect.

It is important to note that from the time Mwanawasa was declared winner, the opposition remained in combative mood. They had tried several methods that they hoped would break Mwanawasa. They had tried to stop him being sworn in. They had tried mass demonstrations. They had also tried to lobby the international community to boycott Mwanawasa. The only realistic one was their petition in the Supreme Court. Thus, the opposition were firing on all cylinders, any of which would have served their purpose.

Its defects notwithstanding, the impeachment motion was significant in Zambia's political history. It was the first such motion to be tabled in Parliament and represented a serious attempt at impeaching the Head of State.

CHAPTER EIGHT

FIGHTING THE CANCER

"History has shown that even those who rose to power with good intentions soon became corrupt. They took advantage of their position to enrich themselves and their family and friends. Then in order to protect their wealth and power, they silenced those who threatened their authority. As one injustice led to another, and as their friends became fewer, they grew increasingly paranoid and oppressive." -**Daniel Kaufmann, former World Bank official and leading expert on governance and development.**

THERE IS A strong body of evidence across the world showing the link between corruption and underdevelopment. It is no coincidence that countries with corrupt governments also lie in the lower league of development.

The 10th United Nations Congress on the Prevention of Crime and Treatment of Offenders, quoting a World Bank survey, noted that more than 150 high-ranking public officials and top citizens from over sixty developing nations ranked corruption as the biggest impediment to economic development and growth in their countries. Corrupt practices drain government coffers, play havoc with free trade and scare away investors. The Bank estimates that corruption can reduce a country's growth rate by 0.5 to 1.0 percentage points per year. Further, International Monetary Fund research has shown that investment in corrupt countries is 5% lower than in countries that are relatively corruption-free.

A more recent study *Corruption from the Perspectives of Citizens, Firms, and Public Officials - Results of Sociological Surveys* (2012) by the World Bank still maintained that corruption was an impediment to economic growth and sustainable development of a country. It reduces the effectiveness of public administration and makes public expenditures inefficient. Most seriously, corruption erodes the rule of law, harms the reputation of the state and weakens citizens' trust in the institutions of state.

In their research, Tanzi and Davoodi (1997) note as follows:

Corruption, particularly political or "grand" corruption, distorts the entire decision-making process connected with public investment projects. Evidence shows that higher corruption is associated with (i) higher public investment (ii) lower government revenues (iii) lower expenditures on operations and maintenance; and (iv) lower quality of public infrastructure.

'Corruption' is not an African word, but the practice is endemic on the continent and is, to a large extent, responsible for its underdevelopment. Why is it that few African leaders leave office with a clean record? Leaders leaving office with a trail of scandals has become the norm rather than the exception. If someone is going to loot billions of state funds, as happened with Zaire's Mobutu Sese Seko and Nigeria's Sani Abacha, then one might ask what time they had to think about developing their countries.

In *Dead Aid*, Dambisa Moyo notes that:

If the world has one picture of African statesmen, it is one of rank corruption on a stupendous scale. There hardly seem any leaders who haven't crowned themselves in gold, seized land, handed over state businesses to relatives and friends, diverted billions to foreign accounts, and generally treated their countries as giant personalised cash dispensers. It's not, of course, just one person who has taken the money. There are many people, at many different levels of the bureaucracy, who have funnelled away billions over the years.

Those governing now and in future have a responsibility to act, and thus, be judged differently. Fighting corruption for any government is not a matter of choice but of necessity.

As the Zambia National Governance Baseline Survey (2004) noted, "…the crusade against corruption…is not a personal or political issue, but a matter of national concern as exhibited by the views of the Zambian population."

The campaign against corruption remains the lasting legacy of Mwanawasa's Presidency. His resignation from government in 1994 was premised as much on his abhorrence for corruption as on his frustrations with being sidelined by Chiluba. He did not agree with the way corruption had become part of the system and his view was that it was being tolerated rather than fought. Therefore, it was not surprising that he made the fight against corruption one of his most important undertakings.

But the irony is that his rise to power was itself stained with corruption. Although the Supreme Court overturned a challenge by the opposition to have his election nullified, the revelations in court about how public funds were used in his campaign left his own integrity and legitimacy in serious question.

Among the witnesses in the petition was Michael Sata, who until September 2001 was national secretary of the MMD. He told the court that the party was broke prior to the election, bringing into question where the MMD found the millions it pumped into its campaign. Vernon Mwaanga, who was MMD national campaign chairperson, testified that the MMD got money from Zesco, the state power utility, to print campaign posters for Mwanawasa. Xavier Chungu, the former head of intelligence, also testified that Chiluba had tasked him to raise money for use in the elections. Money was then stolen from the national intelligence account to purchase MMD campaign vehicles. Chungu narrated how he handed Mwanawasa khaki envelopes containing K200, 000 at State House before the election.

It would have been interesting to know the state of Mwanawasa's conscience regarding the use of public funds to prop up his campaign. He didn't seem to have suffered from reproaches of an accusing conscience. If there was a battle between conscience and ambition, the latter carried the day. But Mwanawasa pleaded ignorance over the allegations of corruption in his election. "For me I don't know that there was corruption. I don't know that the elections were rigged," he argued.

His lawyers did their utmost to reinforce that pleading by distancing him from the theft of public funds. The interpretation was that those who stole the money didn't do it at Mwanawasa's behest and he could not therefore be held responsible for their looting. But, assuming Mwanawasa knew the funds for his campaign were stolen from the national treasury, would he have abandoned the race for the presidency?

After eighty nine days of sitting over a period of three years in which the opposition summoned seventy six witnesses and the State eighty, the punch line from the Supreme Court judgment was:

We are satisfied, on the evidence before us, that the elections, while not being totally perfect as found and discussed, were substantially in conformity with the law and practice. The few partially proved allegations are not indicative that the majority of the voters were prevented from electing the candidate whom they preferred; or that the election was so flawed that the dereliction of duty seriously affected the result which could no longer reasonably be said to reflect the true free choice and free will of the majority of the voters. We, therefore, determine and declare that the 1st Respondent, Levy Patrick Mwanawasa, was duly and validly elected as President of the Republic of Zambia.

Of the thirty six grounds the opposition had advanced against Mwanawasa's election, the court said it "partially proved" three. This was an interesting ruling by the highest court in the land. Law is about precedence. But despite that precedent set by the Supreme Court, Zambians are yet to hear of a judgment from a lower court that would, for instance, find someone to be a 'partial thief' or 'partial drug trafficker' or 'partial rapist'. But such, it seems, is law. It's not an exact science.

While distancing himself from the corruption committed in aid of his election, Mwanawasa's reputation and legitimacy were seriously in jeopardy and he had a responsibility to clear himself from the mess if he was to restore confidence in the entire political and governance system. How he was to do that was no easy task.

Fighting the Cancer

Wholesale plunder reported

While serving as Deputy Minister at State House, Chitala received a bunch of files from a named senior auditor at the Ministry of Finance. "Those files had all the crimes that had been committed in the previous administration," Chitala recollected, shaking his head, seemingly still not believing what had landed on his desk. "My job was to give those files to Mr Mwanawasa. That was the genesis of the fight against corruption."

On 11 July 2002 Mwanawasa summoned a special session of Parliament. It was only the second such session in Zambia's history, the first being in 1967 when Kaunda was faced with a political crisis. The nation wondered what Mwanawasa wanted to say which he had not said earlier in his maiden speech. Apparently, he kept the issues so close to his chest that few in his circle knew what he was going to say. "He had mentioned that he would come to Parliament to make an address on a subject he did not disclose. But I thought whatever it was, it would be significant," said Kavindele, who was then Vice President and Leader of Government business in Parliament.

Zambia watched and listened attentively as Mwanawasa unveiled several allegations of corruption against Chiluba, which later formed the basis for the removal of his presidential immunity. Among the accusations was the 'disappearance' of US$20 million in an arms deal and US$35 million paid by the Binani Group for the purchase of Luanshya mine. In a unanimous decision hailed as a gigantic move against former presidents hiding their crimes behind the cloak of immunity, Parliament waived Chiluba's immunity on 16 July 2002, effectively paving the way for his arrest.

Chiluba protested at being arraigned in Parliament where he said he could not defend himself. He accused Mwanawasa of inciting public hatred against him. Defiantly dismissing the allegations as "a mere figment of imagination lacking in factor or substance", he went up to the Supreme Court to demand his immunity, albeit in vain.

By arresting Chiluba and other ex-government officials, the President delivered a swift statement of intent that the fight against corruption would be one of his major themes of governance and that he would abide by his slogans of 'government of laws and not of men' and 'zero tolerance for corruption'.

Mwanawasa may have had the best of intentions with his anti-corruption crusade, but in some cases, the manner he proceeded gave ammunition to his critics to punch holes into his initiative. For instance, when he addressed the special session of Parliament, he said a *prima facie* case had been established against Chiluba. But what was rather curious was that the numerous allegations he laid before Parliament were never raised as charges when Chiluba was finally prosecuted. Mwanawasa's speech was characterised by figures running into millions of dollars, but the only criminal charge Chiluba was finally prosecuted for was theft of half a million dollars.

What happened to the pile of allegations Mwanawasa took to Parliament? Was he misled as Chiluba and his sympathisers claimed? Did it turn out that there was nothing that amounted to impropriety on Chiluba's part as far as the other allegations were concerned? Was Mwanawasa so overwhelmed by what he found that he didn't apply his highly acclaimed legal mind to check the veracity of issues he took to Parliament? Did his judgment run ahead of the facts? Was it a case of failing to turn a mountain of information into a legally compelling narrative? Or was it incompetence by the people he entrusted with the task?

I put these questions to lawyers and non-lawyers alike.

"The ideal situation would have been to investigate those allegations," Kavindele argued. "My view is that the action was not genuine because he failed to prove the allegations against Chiluba."

Chitala thought Mwanawasa had done his part by bringing out the issues and it was then up to the prosecutors to deliver. "I don't know why the DPP and the Task Force failed," he said, but added, with a concession, "investigating white collar crime is not easy."

"Being a legal mind, he was not comfortable with throwing everything to the courts," a Lusaka lawyer told me, innocuously suggesting that perhaps Mwanawasa eventually sifted through what could stand in court. "In a criminal matter you need evidence beyond reasonable doubt."

Another lawyer told me: "I had the same questions. I really don't know what happened. I met him twice when he was President but we didn't have enough time to discuss that."

When I asked Nalumango where Mwanawasa failed in his Presidency, she took a long pause and then said, "Not enough was done to bring Chiluba to account for some of his cases." She said "not enough" was done in sensitising Members of Parliament on what the issues were. Considering how close Mwanawasa kept the issues to himself and how fast-paced the events played out in that one week, "not enough" was even an overstatement. There was simply no sensitisation that took place. "When the issue of Chiluba came to Parliament, many of us were new in the House, we didn't know what was happening," Nalumango acknowledged.

Mwaanga carries the distinction of having worked closely with four presidents. He is something of a presidential encyclopaedia. In his memoirs, he says the outgoing administration briefed Mwanawasa's ministers on some of the issues he took to Parliament, specifically the arms deal and the sale of Luanshya mine. Mwaanga is short of saying the issues were straightforward. However, as a consummate insider, he does not say whether the ministers in turn briefed Mwanawasa and what his reaction may have been. So, if Mwaanga is right, and assuming the ministers passed on the information to their boss, then it leaves us with two options: either to question why Mwanawasa went ahead with his allegations, or to conclude that he was not satisfied with what he was told.

In the final analysis, however, it is immaterial whether Mwanawasa and his ministers were briefed because, in the end, several of Chiluba's henchmen – ranging from top military generals to key treasury officials and private individuals – were all proved to have looted state funds and were convicted accordingly. That the majority of the issues Mwanawasa raised in Parliament never made it on Chiluba's charge sheet remains a glaring question (and perhaps that's where Mwaanga could be right), but Mwanawasa's overall suspicion with what happened under Chiluba's government was justified as exemplified by some of the convictions secured.

Not the ACC, but the Task Force

After arraigning Chiluba, Mwanawasa formed a 'Task Force on Corruption' to probe the plunder. Mwanawasa's decision to establish such a body, when various other state institutions already existed for that purpose, was heavily criticised as an act of undermining the same institutions he swore to protect. The mandate of the Task Force was limited to investigating cases in the Chiluba era. It lacked a legal framework to guide its operations and merely subsisted on the strength of the President's executive powers. Numerous calls from civil society and the opposition that the Task Force be regularised, to give it some legal backing, were ignored. The Task Force was financially and logistically well enough off to perform its duties, as Mwanawasa had sourced millions of dollars from donors for its operations.

But the Anti-Corruption Commission (ACC), with its broader mandate and sound legal backing, continued to be underfunded. Yet Mwanawasa had the bizarre courage to publicly castigate the ACC by accusing it of not doing enough to fight corruption. Such a position was woefully contradictory. How did he expect the ACC to fight corruption when at that stage all eyes (and almost all funding) were on the almighty Task Force? While the Task Force was limited to investigating corruption of the Chiluba era, who was to probe corruption in Mwanawasa's administration? The same poorly resourced ACC which Mwanawasa frequently antagonised.

Mwanawasa had won an emphatic seal of approval from donors as far as fighting corruption was concerned. Ideally, that should have put him in a unique position to direct the crusade. That was not to be. The creation of the Task Force alienated the ACC from its core mandate. The Task Force became more famous than the ACC. But what was really special about cases of the Chiluba era? An examination of them shows that they were mainly two types - theft by public servant and abuse of office. So what was it about these two types of offences that the ACC could not deal with? The Task Force in part comprised ACC officers seconded to it. Further, donors had previously funded the ACC and the Drug Enforcement Commission with millions of dollars over a long period of time. Why did they now not have confidence in the very institutions they had massively invested in over a long time?

Mwanawasa was indebted to donors for the funding. But that indebtedness should not have gone to the level of undermining state institutions. There was no need, for instance, for him to sign a Memorandum of Understanding with donors to the point of including provisions to have a selected list of magistrates to handle cases prosecuted by the Task Force.

For instance, Article 2.5 of the MoU stated that:

The successful prosecution of these cases will depend to a large extent on the integrity and competence of the magistrate assigned to handle the cases. It will be beneficial to have a few of the best magistrates designated to handle all the cases brought by the Task Force...

It was partly for the above reason that those prosecuted under this crusade argued it was a predetermined, donor-driven agenda and a ploy by Mwanawasa to shine before the international community. But that view is too simplistic given the broader context of corruption in Chiluba's administration. It is public knowledge that donors were charmed by Mwanawasa's campaign; they had found an ally who was willing to go the full mile and in response they provided the funding. It's also true that many mistakes were made in that crusade and no one should dare claim it was flawless. But that does not mean those prosecuted and convicted under the work of the Task Force were in fact clean. They were not.

The Task Force caused quite some confusion among law enforcement officers. Notwithstanding its questionable legal status, it should have been answerable to the Director of Public Prosecutions (DPP), but instead reported directly to Mwanawasa. This created animosity between officers who had direct access to the President and the DPP whose authority was undermined. As a lawyer, Mwanawasa knew what the procedure was. So what had happened to the DPP, the supervisor of all prosecutors acting for the state?

In his book *A Mockery of Justice*, Chiluba's former press secretary, Richard Sakala, gives a detailed account of what he characterises as lawlessness on the part of the Task Force. In reference to one of his cases, Sakala narrates that, although the magistrate confirmed that the DPP had given consent to prosecute him and his co-accused with the offence of abuse of authority of office, the Task Force illegally replaced that with a charge of theft of motor vehicle, a non-bailable offence. The latter was what Sakala and his colleagues were prosecuted for, and not the charge preferred by the DPP.

The Task Force had its faithful worshippers and high priests who refused to admit its flaws and placed it on a very high moral ground. But what Sakala shares in his book cannot merely be dismissed as the bitter feelings of an ex-convict; it offers an insight into the behind-the-scenes intrigue and feuds in the highly acclaimed fight against corruption.

In reference to the competing players, Sakala writes:

What further compounded the situation [of his impending prosecution] was the multiplicity of institutions involved in the criminal justice system. One group was led by Mark Chona and Mutembo Nchito, private citizens recruited to ostensibly help in the prosecution of corruption, while the other was led by Minister of Legal Affairs and Attorney General, George Kunda, and the then Director of Public Prosecutions (DPP), Mukelabai Mukelabai. Between them there seemed to be a bad feeling and for those of us in their sights, the situation was grim and dire. If my case was to be prosecuted by the DPP, I stood a fighting chance. Mukelabai was impartial and not influenced by the President. However, I felt if I was to be prosecuted by Mutembo Nchito, I would fall under the parallel "private" prosecution system where everything was possible, in which case my chances were limited. The existence of two prosecution authorities was a matter of great concern.

Mwanawasa stuck to his guns and defended the Task Force and its operations.

The slow pace at which it prosecuted cases was a matter he had regularly expressed dissatisfaction about, although he did appreciate the complexity of investigating and prosecuting such cases, some of them stretching across continents. But his patience with the Task Force ran thin and his frustration blew up when he hinted at abolishing it shortly after winning re-election, accusing it of "dismal performance," a statement Task Force supporters found hard to swallow.

"From my interaction with him, he didn't regret creating the Task Force but he felt it didn't perform to his satisfaction and that it didn't achieve what he wanted," Nalumango revealed.

According to Kavindele, he had asked Mwanawasa why he formed the Task Force instead of using the ACC. His response was "Those were appointed by Chiluba and cannot do a good job."

But the manner in which the Task Force carried out its work undermined its credibility and reflected badly on the chief crusader. Key suspects disappeared from under its nose. Former spy chief and Chiluba's alleged partner in crime, Xavier Chungu jumped bail and fled the country in unexplained circumstances. From the time he was arrested, Chungu had been under surveillance, senior security officials said. But how he eluded the dragnet remains a mystery.

Zambia's former Ambassador to the USA, Attan Shansonga, another suspect who was also facing corruption charges, fooled the Task Force into facilitating his travel to the United Kingdom, supposedly to collect evidence to pin down Chiluba and his other associates. You surely do not need to be very intelligent to question the wisdom of sending a suspect on a mission to collect evidence for his own crimes. To create fertile ground for the belief that Shansonga had bolted, the Task Force cooked up a story and even had the strange courage to call a press briefing to announce that he was spotted in a taxi in the southern border town of Siavonga. What an attempt to cover up a gaffe.

Shansonga's trip to the UK was sanctioned by the Task Force. They discussed it with him; they bought him an air ticket and put him on a UK-bound plane. How could he then find himself in Siavonga? Even more imprudent was

Zambia's request to London to extradite Shansonga, someone they willingly let off the hook but were now pretending to be sweating to bring within their ambit. As the plane taxied, you wonder what Shansonga must have thought of the Task Force. He might have looked through the window, not believing his luck, then shaking his head and laughing at their gullibility before smacking them in the face. He never returned – only an idiot would.

Such clumsy operations by the Task Force were a huge indictment on its performance, a major setback to the anti-corruption crusade and a frustration to Mwanawasa, given his public show of eagerness to tackle graft.

Further, as a body that showed enormous zeal to probe corruption, the Task Force should have been above board in its operations. But it was failing to meet the standards it was expecting of people it was investigating. The Auditor General revealed rampant misuse of funds, including lack of care for recovered properties. Not even prosecutors were engaged according to the law, the auditors found out. I asked Mark Chona, former Executive Chairman of the Task Force, to respond to these issues. He declined.

However, despite its sometimes dubious decisions, squabbles with other law enforcement agencies, its own failures at accountability and other shortfalls, the Task Force was successful in recording some convictions. From bank executives to top military generals and senior treasury officials, all were found wanting for dipping their fingers in the public purse. This corrupt bunch could not blame the inadequacies of the Task Force for the situation they found themselves in. They were appropriately paying for their abuse of state power.

Return it, I will pardon you

Less than a week after Chiluba's immunity was lifted, Mwanawasa pledged to pardon him if he returned what he allegedly pocketed. He said: "All I can say is that I am anxious to advance the cause of the nation. If Dr Chiluba comes to me and says 'this is the money I took from the people of Zambia, I am returning it,' then I am prepared to be crucified by the people of Zambia."

How could pardoning suspects "advance the cause of the nation"? Why was

Mwanawasa "prepared to be crucified by the people of Zambia" for crimes he was sure lay squarely in Chiluba's lap? How could he, on the one hand, declare that he wanted Chiluba to face the law, and on the other, promise to pardon him even before the court process ran its course?

It is not for the President to cut deals with the indicted on whatever terms. It's for them to prove their innocence in court. Assuming the separation of powers truly exists in Zambia, it would be against the principle for the President to interfere in the work of the Judiciary by promising to pardon suspects whose fate lies before the courts. As many had cared to ask, how was Mwanawasa going to tell the actual amount of the loot if indeed Chiluba met the other end of the bargain? Chiluba was not amused by that offer and, in fact, protested at Mwanawasa's remarks.

In response to accusations that he had concentrated too much on pursuing corruption of the past while similar scandals rocked his administration, Mwanawasa countered with some instant dismissals of public officials accused of corruption and used that measure as a warning to the would-be corrupt. But his decision to allow some members of his own party who were in court on corruption charges to remain in leadership worked against his openly expressed desire to rid public institutions of corruption. The question his critics asked was: how is he going to fight corruption on a larger scale when he tolerates suspects in his own club?

Staunch legalist he was, Mwanawasa went for the maxim: innocent until proven guilty. Based on this, he even retained in public office people that had been acquitted, saying if the courts had cleared them, who was he to stick a filthy tag on them? This argument was legally sound. However, what was in question was the moral, rather than the legal element. While the courts could clear them, having them back in public offices would only expose them to suspicion, as society would still have a murky picture of their integrity.

Bulaya: not too far off the hook

Dr Kashiwa Bulaya was a former Permanent Secretary in the Ministry of

Health. He had been arrested in 2003 for abuse of office and corrupt practices involving K3 million meant for AIDS drugs. As the case progressed, the state dropped it in May 2005 on the grounds that it was "not in the public interest." For two years, prosecutors were convinced of Bulaya's corruption. How his prosecution suddenly turned out to be against public interest was inexplicable. The decision backfired and was a source of embarrassment to Mwanawasa. The diplomatic community, civil society and the opposition took turns in condemning government.

Although Justice Minister George Kunda, and Director of Public Prosecutions Chalwe Mchenga laboured to exonerate Mwanawasa from any personal interference in the case, it failed to calm the waters. Bulaya had testified in Mwanawasa's favour in the presidential petition. His release from prosecution was therefore widely construed as a 'payback' for his favourable testimony. While the President personally may not supervise his appointees so strictly, it's difficult to imagine how officers who serve at his pleasure could be allowed to engage in acts that undermined his image and integrity, especially for a man whose position on corruption was so well known.

Zambians who speculated that the discontinuation of Bulaya's case could not have been done without Mwanawasa's knowledge could be forgiven. If he wasn't aware, then his subordinates acted behind his back, which brings into question where they got the excess latitude and whose interest they were serving in making such a reckless decision.

Initially, government stood its ground, hoping the issue would die down. Civil society and the media piled pressure and the case was reinstated. This was a classic example of what a social coalition of civil society and the media could do to keep the government in check.

When Bulaya was found guilty and sentenced to five years imprisonment in 2007, those who opposed the discontinuation of his case stood vindicated as champions of justice, while Mwanawasa and his group were indicted in the public eye. The conclusion is that Bulaya would never have been successfully prosecuted had there not been such a strong opposition to machinations to

Left: *Elias Chipimo (senior), Chiluba and Mwanawasa campaigning in 1991.*

Centre left: *Family time in the Mfuwe game park.*

Centre right: *A moment of romance after Mwanawasa was bestowed with an Honorary Doctorate in Law at Harding Universiy in the US.*

Bottom: *Mwanawasa and Chiluba at the airport to receive remains of the Gabon Air Crash victims.*

Top Left: *Being congratulated by Justice Minister George Kunda and aide Ben Kapita for the Honorary Doctorate in Law at Harding University in the US.*

Above: *Mr Integrity - The fight against corruption remains his outstanding legacy.*

Left: *The impeachment motion was no threat to the tough talker.*

Below: *Mwanawasa and Sata meet at the Cathedral of the Holy Cross.*

Top: *Although Mwanawasa made tremendous strides in reforming the Legislature, there is still need for more work to make it truly democratic and acccountable.*

Right: *If Mwanawasa had delivered the constitution, his legacy would have been enhanced.*

Left: *Despite the smiles and handshakes, Mwanawasa took a hard line against his southern neighbour.*

Bottom: *Zambia has seen it all with constitution-making.*

Above: *Thabo Mbeki and Mwanawasa saw things in Zimbabwe differently.*

Left: *Rupiah Banda - the outsider found in the right place.*

Bottom: *Farewell Mwanawasa.*

let him off the hook. Clearly, decisions such as returning favours to people who were caught on the wrong end of the law should never have come from a government that had vowed to fight corruption in all its facets, regardless of who was involved.

Red carpet for Katumbi

When Mwanawasa indicted Chiluba, he named several other individuals suspected to have been his collaborators. Among them was Moses Katumbi, a Congolese businessman with close links to Chiluba. Investigators pursued Katumbi, firmly believing he was Chiluba's partner in crime. But that zeal collapsed some five years later. In December 2007, after the Zambia-Democratic of Republic of Congo Joint Permanent Commission in Lubumbashi where Katumbi was now governor, Zambia's Attorney General Mumba Malila announced that Zambia and Katumbi had reached a "mutual agreement" to stop court cases they had against each other. Furthermore Katumbi, who had been on the Zambian wanted list, was now free to enter the country and do business again.

Amid mounting criticism, government said it was no longer correct to continue pursuing Katumbi as that was detrimental to diplomatic ties with a neighbouring country. Diplomatic relations between the two countries were never in doubt and even as the government repeatedly told the nation how determined it was to arrest Katumbi if he ever set foot on Zambian soil, it knew of the need for good neighbourliness and warm diplomatic relations. The decision to drop charges against Katumbi had nothing to do with diplomacy or good neighbourliness but to the secret deals that were struck behind closed doors in the Togolese capital, Lome where the two parties met. Mwaanga reveals that when he met Katumbi in Lubumbashi in March 2007, he had expressed his desire to drop his court cases if Zambia stopped pursuing him. Therefore, it can be concluded that this deal was the consummation of that desire. Isn't it also interesting that two friendly neighbouring parties had to go to West Africa just to agree to drop each other's demands?

It was a weekend of high drama. While on his way to Lisbon for the EU-Africa Summit, Mwanawasa stopped over in Berlin where he told Zambians there how disappointed he was with the ACC at their slow pace of handling cases. Back home in Lusaka, the Attorney General was announcing a deal with a suspect it had vowed to bring to book. Elsewhere in the capital, Justice Minister George Kunda, officiating at the United Nations Anti-Corruption Day, was recommitting the administration to a tougher fight against corruption; all this in one weekend. It was such actions that rather discoloured Mwanawasa's fight against corruption.

Like the walls of Jericho?

The reckless theft of public funds under a government that exhibited an enormous abhorrence for corruption was a damning indictment. Each year the Auditor General's report revealed blatant disregard for the use of taxpayers' money. The problem was perennially endemic and cut across the entire civil service and quasi-government institutions. For instance, between 2001 and 2005, the treasury lost K14.7 billion. This was a scam of gigantic scale. Ineffective internal control systems and lack of remedial measures only aided civil servants in further pilfering public funds. While the theft of public funds continued on an immense scale, the establishment was awash with the rhetoric of "fiscal discipline." Whenever the public queried why development projects were not being implemented, government pleaded lack of funds. Yet, colossal sums of money disappeared while people were denied services.

By failing to stem the theft of public funds and also failing to deal firmly with thieving civil servants, the government discredited itself, notwithstanding its anti-corruption rhetoric. That inaction sent word to others that you could steal public funds and get away with it. Although the levels of financial morality collapsed under Chiluba, there was a limit to which Mwanawasa could blame the past. He was in charge and was obliged to act against the theft of funds if his zest to fight corruption was to be taken seriously. Unless he also dealt with corruption in his own system, critics would have cause to feel justified in their charge that he was using his crusade as a smokescreen for his own administration. Financial scandals in government continued on, as revealed by successive reports of the Auditor General.

Mwanawasa's anti-corruption campaign suffered many knocks, but it also secured laudable successes which showed that the efforts were worthwhile. For instance, as stated earlier, all of Chiluba's corrupt defence chiefs and his other collaborators were sent to jail. Their convictions were not by coincidence but a clear sign that there was a systematic scheme in place to loot the country. It also smacked of a systemic failure of leadership on Chiluba's part.

High on the list of achievements on this subject was the London High Court ruling against Chiluba and nineteen others. In the civil case Zambia took to the court, Justice Peter Smith ruled that Chiluba and others conspired to defraud Zambia of US$46 million. The judgment, though only symbolic as it was eventually never registered in Zambia to be effective, was a plus to Mwanawasa's crusade considering that people had been calling for results. As Chiluba's case in Lusaka slowed down due to legal technicalities and his ill health, the London court found him wanting. It was a damning judgment in every respect. It not only examined the case at hand but also denounced Chiluba's character and lifestyle.

Smith was quite graphic in his choice of words. In paragraphs 25 to 29 of the judgment's executive summary, he states:

The most telling example of corruption was the clothing acquired by FJT [Chiluba]. He had a worldwide reputation as being a smart and expensive dresser. He had his own stylish suits with his initials (FJT) monogrammed on them, a large number of specially made signature shoes and literally thousands of monogrammed shirts. As President he earned about $105,000 over 10 years. Yet an exclusive shop in Switzerland (Basile) received $1,200,000. AGZ [Attorney General of Zambia] established the entirety of this was stolen from the Republic mostly via the use of the secret Zamtrop Account which had been set

> up and controlled by XFC [Xavier Frank Chungu] under the personal supervision of FJT. **This was at a time when the vast majority of Zambians were struggling to live on $1 a day and many could not afford more than 1 meal a day** (Smith's own emphasis).
>
> Just under $500,000 was apparently spent on clothes for the FJT; the rest is completely unaccounted for. FJT had the benefit of this largesse at the expense of the people of Zambia. He still wears some of the clothes. He has had numerous opportunities to explain this to the Zambian people but he has failed to do so. There is no evidence to show FJT had the personal wealth to buy these clothes. Nor is there evidence contrary to statements he made to the press that it was funded by gifts paid into the Zamtrop account. It was simply stolen from the Republic. **The people of Zambia should know that whenever he appears in public wearing some of these clothes he acquired them with money stolen from them** (Smith's own emphasis).

Donors, who had pumped millions of dollars into the crusade and who had always called for accountability in the use of their aid, were elated by the judgment. In a joint statement, the major Western donors – Britain, Denmark, Ireland, Norway, the Netherlands, Sweden and the USA – stated:

> It is courageous that the Government of Zambia has pursued this case and that a former head of State has been held accountable for corrupt activities in this way. This is likely to have an impact on corruption in Africa and globally. The judgment decreed that Dr Chiluba returns State funds misappropriated from the Government's ZAMTROP (Intelligence) account during his term of office. We jointly welcome the judgment as an historic victory for the people of Zambia that shows their commitment to bring those who steal from the State to account regardless of how powerful they are. We look forward to a further institutionalisation of the fight against high-level corruption in Zambia.

Fighting the Cancer

But Chiluba rejected the judgment and accused Mwanawasa and British Prime Minister Tony Blair of corruption and "imperialist conspiracy" against him. He dismissed Judge Smith's ruling as corrupt and racist. He charged that Mwanawasa's and Blair's fight against corruption had "collapsed like the walls of Jericho."

"It is my opinion that both gentlemen – Tony Blair and Mr Mwanawasa – advanced the popular slogan of corruption to hide their own skeletons in cupboards. They have not provided the necessary leadership they pontificated. Though not a lawyer, I find this judgment unacceptable and therefore reject it," Chiluba said in his silky accent.

Chiluba's strenuous rejection of the judgment didn't change the overwhelming perception that he had abused his position of trust. He stood condemned in the public eye with his reputation substantially ragged. Two years later, he was acquitted by the Lusaka court in his other case. But why and how Chiluba, the chief suspect and supposed master of the art, managed to escape jail is a subject for another book.

By providing the right leadership, a President is best placed to make what he wants his government to be. By his conduct and that of his subordinates, he can make it everyone's pride or anyone's disdain. It would be nice to have a President who prevented corruption and theft of public funds and implanted a great sense of responsibility in all the people working in the administration. However, given the complex structure of government, plus some workers who may not share this zeal, even with a President's best intentions, it may be not possible and one will still have some bad eggs spoiling the omelette. British Labour Party politician, Harriet Harman once said, "Not all civil servants admire strong political leadership. But if you want to change things for the better you need strong political leadership."

All must account

Credit should be given to Mwanawasa for managing to raise corruption as a key governance issue that must be tackled head-on. Many of the corruption cases that went to court involving former high profile public officials could not have arisen without Mwanawasa. Under his leadership, there was recognition of corruption as an evil, 'a cancer', as he called it. The fact that corruption featured heavily in most governance issues demonstrated that Mwanawasa's message had struck a chord. He must also be credited for taking a bold decision that showed no one was above the law. If he ensured that the man who gave him the presidency faced the law, theoretically no one could expect kinder treatment. He did set a precedent that it is not right for a succeeding president – whether from the same party or not and whether handpicked or popularly elected – to sweep dirt under the carpet in the name of maintaining favourable relations with his predecessor even when he reasonably suspects wrongdoing. He demonstrated that it does not matter who you are – you can be called to account as the law deems. Public good must always override personal considerations. The risk was high, but the dividend was worth it.

Surveys by Transparency International Zambia revealed that in 2002 77% of the respondents believed Mwanawasa was handling the fight against corruption more seriously than his predecessor. In 2004, however, the proportion that held that view had declined to 60%. Based on its findings the survey concluded: "It is evident that there is general disillusionment with current corruption trends. There is also growing perception that although the Mwanawasa's government is seriously committed to the fight against corruption, most people still feel not much is being achieved."

Various reasons could be advanced for that change in perception, among which could be the inconsistencies highlighted earlier.

Mwanawasa was determined to fight corruption. Going by his pronouncements, it is something he felt very strongly about. "He warned everyone who worked with him that if you were found wanting, he would not protect you," Kalala recalled. While on an official government trip Nalumango attended to some party activities. On her return Mwanawasa asked her to refund part of the money. Several ministers were prosecuted and convicted of various offences.

Fighting the Cancer

But sometimes he seems to have felt he was a loner in the crusade. This explains why, on numerous occasions, he publicly told his ministers to speak out against corruption. Unsurprisingly, his strong views on corruption formed the bulk of his farewell speech which he recorded three years before he died. Did his circle believe in what he believed or were they just pretenders? Only the future would tell.

While Mwanawasa did a lot to advance the fight against corruption, it is also true that he committed errors of judgment either on his own or at the advice of his inner circle – the men and women who closely surrounded him. However, it can be said he did an honest job as his crusade uncovered several issues and provided some valuable lessons.

Firstly, it showed how dishonest those entrusted with the management of public affairs could be. It revealed that leaders could abrogate the social contract entered into with the people. It was an eye opener into what goes on in government and the governed should be on guard.

Secondly, it opened a new chapter on governance in Zambia in that those who assume public office will be under tight scrutiny to ensure that what happened in the past is prevented as citizens would now be more vigilant. This has clearly been evidenced by the outrage that accompanies reported cases of corruption in government.

Thirdly, it helped explain why Zambia ranked low on the development index as resources that were to benefit the entire country went into the pockets of a greedy few.

Lastly, that if you are going to fight corruption, your actions must be above board and consistent with your pronouncements.

CHAPTER NINE

GOVERNANCE OF LAWS AND LOWS

"Democracy, good governance and modernity cannot be imported or imposed from outside a country." - **Emile Lahud, President of Lebanon, 1998 - 2007.**

LIKE AN ACCIDENT, good governance does not just happen. It has to be caused. Democracy by itself is incapable of guaranteeing good governance nor can it necessarily be a by-product of the former. History the world over shows that even popular governments elected on an impressively sound democratic footing can turn tyrannical and consign the people who elected them to untold misrule. It is good to have 'good people' run government. But it is not enough. Strong systems and institutions are required to buffer the state. However, dictators and demagogues always have a way of manipulating even the most robust systems and institutions. When this happens, it is a call to the masses to rise and stave off such manoeuvres.

It is no secret that Mwanawasa was quite contemptuous of Chiluba's governance record. Despite leading a party that promised massive reforms relating to good governance, Chiluba abysmally fell short. Kaunda had his deficits as far as governance was concerned. The perennial State of Emergency, the curtailing of civil liberties, detentions and torture of political opponents, limited political space and restricted media freedom characterised Kaunda's rule. Chiluba committed the MMD to a fundamental shift. Flattered with the honour of leading a nation, he soon discarded the eloquence with which he promised to offer better governance. It became his obsession to brutalise those he did not agree with. Enemies – real or imaginary – were on the receiving end of his vindictiveness, while state institutions became his tools for advancing personal causes. So insidious was Chiluba's failure at good governance that donors had to freeze aid to compel him to change.

Both the Munyama and Banda Commissions indicted Chiluba's human rights record. But typical of its wanton insolence, his government never bothered to act on the recommendations of the two Commissions. Rather than dismissing officers whom the Banda Commission named as violators of human rights, Chiluba instead promoted the culprits. A President who had promised respect for human rights, who swore to defend and uphold the Constitution was having no troubled conscience rewarding impunity through the promotion of reprobates. This slap in the face of the Commission had become Chiluba's way of conducting affairs of the state. It had become characteristic of him to appoint Commissions of Inquiry at great expense to the taxpayer, the findings of which he had no intention of respecting.

Chiluba was also known for meddling in the judiciary. An example was his suspension of High Court judge Kabazo Chanda after he overruled the Speaker's decision to try and sentence journalists of *The Post* newspaper. The judge ruled that Parliament was not a court. In another act, justice Chanda had released prisoners who had been in custody for years without charge. That did not go down well with Chiluba. The private media had their gruesome share of Chiluba's clampdown in his bid to keep a tight grip on power.

The foregoing were just a few examples of what was part of the governance record that Chiluba bequeathed his successor. Mwanawasa had to show cause for people to judge him differently. He had differences with his political opponents whom he occasionally threatened. But he was nowhere near the scandalous scale of Kaunda and Chiluba, separately or combined.

Opening the House

Mwanawasa instituted several measures aimed at improving the governance system. The reforms introduced were either aimed at reinforcing existing institutions and laws or creating new ones to keep up with the changes and exigencies of a democracy. The following is not an exhaustive list.

We set off with parliamentary reforms. In his book *The Parliament of Zambia*, former Clerk of the National Assembly, Mwelwa Chibesakunda, observed that, "With the fast growing political awareness among the populace, there has been a corresponding demand for more information on Parliament. There has been a need for Government to take Parliament closer to the people with a view to facilitating a mature construction and assessment of its deliberations."

The need to open up Parliament and take it "closer to the people" was long overdue. While Zambia had embraced a free and open society in the name of democracy, the operations of one of the key institutions of governance remained backward. By electing Members of Parliament, Zambians deposit their power into Parliament to deliberate over the affairs of the nation. It was, therefore, ironic that an institution that exists for and belongs to the people solely for their welfare could be shrouded in some very unnecessary secrecy and governed by discriminatory laws.

For instance, the dress code at Parliament remained elitist. To deny citizens access to Parliament because they could not afford a tie and a jacket or any such equivalent apparel in the case of women was distancing the people from governance. The relaxation of the dress code and allowing the public to enter the House and follow its business was a tremendous change. The establishment of a radio station broadcasting live proceedings to several parts of the country enabled the electorate to access the business in the Legislature.

Previously, and in keeping with its eerie custom of being more of a sacred shrine and less of a public institution, Parliament didn't allow the media and the public into Parliamentary Committees. But following the reforms, information that had been confined to the beautiful fortifications of Parliament was now in the public domain.

The establishment of constituency offices for MPs was also part of the reforms that helped address the gap between representatives and the governed. Where such offices exist, citizens are no longer required to wait for their MP to return from parliamentary sittings before they can share their concerns, as they can now be channelled through the MP's office. It is interesting to note that the need to have offices for MPs was among the recommendations made by the Chona Commission in 1972, but that recommendation did not see the light of day.

However, despite these reforms, Parliament remained largely a rubber stamp of the Executive. (I know that inside the Zambian Parliament, 'rubber stamp' is deemed 'unparliamentary' but I am not an MP, so I am at liberty). Where members of the Executive are also members of the Legislature, it's obvious that whatever the former want to push through the latter, they will more often than not have their way. Thus the oversight role of Parliament is diluted. However, this cannot be blamed on Mwanawasa, as it was a system he inherited as provided for in the Constitution. It is for this reason that some have advocated for the appointment of Cabinet from outside Parliament to enhance the separation of powers. Those opposed to such a system obviously want the status quo to continue, where the Executive uses Parliament merely to legitimise its decisions, no matter how rash.

The Auditor General's Office is another key institution in the governance of the country. It's the public's right to know how their funds are expended. While the Treasury allocates funds to each public institution and is obliged to know how that money is spent, the broader mandate of tracking such expenditure falls on the Auditor General's Office. Auditing public institutions helps to show how public money has been expended and whether such expenditure was used for the intended purpose and in line with established rules and procedures. It also ensures that those who abuse taxpayers' money are exposed and that corrective measures are taken.

Before Mwanawasa, the Auditor General's reports took time to be tabled before Parliament and in such cases it was possible that queries raised in the reports could be overtaken by time and circumstance. And given the 'closed' nature of Parliament then, it is no wonder that the public never really got to know what answers culprits provided to the Public Accounts Committee. Mwanawasa strengthened and expanded the office to provincial level. It made remarkable progress both in the frequency and timeliness of reports. That it had found its long lost feet was not in doubt following the many audit queries it raised on how huge sums of public funds had been misapplied.

Once the Auditor General's report is published and placed before Parliament, controlling officers in government institutions are called to answer audit queries. With the reforms at Parliament, it meant the media could cover sessions of the Public Accounts Committee discussing the report. This provided the public with information on how their money was being spent (or misapplied and stolen as is largely the case). Public outrage over the misuse of public funds was a direct result of access to such information as uncovered by the Auditor General's Office and reported by the media. Mwanawasa should be credited for raising the profile of the Auditor General's Office. But the most vexing issue remained the limitation of its powers. It has no powers to punish, culprits largely go scot free and almost the same audit queries recur every year.

Remain in your palaces

The role of the traditional leadership in governance has for some time been a contested one. One school of thought is that chiefs belong to the traditional side of society and should not contaminate their advisory role by involving themselves in politics. But there has also been concern that chiefs are merely relegated to traditional figureheads with very little influence on governance matters. Although the Chona Commission is better known for recommending the introduction of the one party state, it did cover a number of other governance issues. For instance, on the role of chiefs in governance, the Commission reported, inter alia:

> *An overwhelming number of petitioners who spoke on this issue submitted that chiefs should have more powers and therefore more influence than at present. It was for this reason that some petitioners suggested that matters relating to chiefs should be conducted along the pre-Independence lines with chiefs presiding in court and their Kapasos [retainers] arresting criminals. Other views expressed were for chiefs*

> *to be represented in Parliament; the retention of an enlarged House of Chiefs with power to veto bills; more involvement of chiefs on District Development Committees; Provincial Development Committees and Rural Councils; powers to approve applications for firearms and for business licences; the settling of local customary disputes out of court; more administrative powers for chiefs at village level and control of movement of people from rural to urban areas. A few in this group even suggested that chiefs should be accorded government ministerial status in matters of housing, transport, etc. A few petitioners, however, called for the abolition of chieftainship because they felt that chiefs received public funds for doing nothing.*

The 1996 Constitution barred chiefs from participating in politics, so did the one initiated by Mwanawasa. It would seem that for Mwanawasa one way of reconciling these interests was to have an institution where chiefs could discuss matters of development both in their own areas and the nation in general. This was in view of the contention that it was improper for chiefs to engage in politics as their role was to provide leadership in a non-partisan manner. Hence, Mwanawasa revived the House of Chiefs which had been dormant for a long time. This move was somewhat of a stabiliser of calls for chiefs' involvement in politics.

However, the reintroduction of the House of Chiefs did not stop chiefs from aligning themselves with political parties of their choice. Whilst, theoretically, chiefs are expected to be non-partisan, they too are political animals who have been known to show their colours when it matters. As with many other issues of a public nature, the position of politicians on chiefs' involvement in politics is never a definite one. When a chief supports party X, leaders of that political outfit receive the support with both hands, but when that chief turns to party Y, the chief is castigated for 'straying' and accused of dividing his subjects.

Local government is a key aspect of the national governance system. While the central government should be concerned with the aggregate good of the country, local government should plan for and spearhead development activities at local level. The proposition is that locals know their needs better than the bureaucrat in the national capital. The launch of the National Decentralisation Policy in 2005 was an indication that the much talked about reforms in local government were in sight. Through the implementation of the policy, decision-making would move "from the centre to the periphery." The policy envisaged that the devolution of power to local authorities would enhance the implementation of development programmes and citizens would have a greater say in governance.

Although the policy was markedly ambitious, it would only achieve its purpose through implementation. Key to the implementation was improving service delivery in municipalities whose capacity leaves much to be desired. The capacity of most municipalities in the country remains awfully weak. If they fail to provide municipal services such as garbage collection, water and sanitation, good roads, and, most of all, fail to meet their wage bills, it is anyone's guess how they would execute tasks under the policy. The reluctance by bureaucrats in central government to surrender certain functions to the district is another factor that threatens policy implementation. This tendency would take time to break, considering that for many years, decision making in Zambia's governance system has been highly centralised.

But the greatest threat to the policy was that five years after its launch and establishment of a secretariat, the Decentralisation Implementation Plan (DIP), which was supposed to operationalise the policy, was stuck in Cabinet. One diplomat whose government was involved in funding the implementation once told me that there was resistance to the policy from the higher echelons, mainly on account of fear of losing control of decision-making. Consequently, the donor could not spend their money. Whether this policy - with its ambitious objectives that essentially aimed at restructuring the local government system – would take off and its results seen, was a matter where only time will tell.

Police have a crucial role in the maintenance of law and order. But this is one institution that has been plagued with serious difficulties ranging from inadequate funding, corruption, to lack of respect for human rights. The establishment of the Police Public Complaints Authority and the Professional Standards Unit within the Police Service was aimed at giving an opportunity to the citizenry to report erring officers to the two institutions for remedial action. To what extent these institutions have been able to cure the mischief is not known. It is good to establish institutions that enhance governance but such institutions must not exist in name only. They must not only be seen to work, they must work and produce results. It is also incumbent upon citizens to ensure that they utilise to the maximum institutions that are created to serve them. However, despite having such institutions, incidents of extrajudicial killings and torturing of suspects by law enforcement officers continued as many human rights reports showed, casting a bad light on the government's human rights record.

The Judicial Complaints Authority was set up to deal with complaints of misconduct of judicial officers brought by members of the public. The extent to which the success of such institutions can be measured also depends on how the public utilise the institutions. The government and the agencies themselves need to do more to enlighten citizens about the role of such bodies. It does not matter how noble and clearly laid out their functions are, if the citizenry remain ignorant, those institutions can go to sleep.

No hangman

Zambia's human rights record under Mwanawasa saw some improvement. Oppression of dissent was not part of the order compared to the Kaunda and Chiluba regimes where some political opponents were arrested, detained and tortured at the hands of the State on trumped up charges. Mwanawasa's record does not exhibit any systematic attempt to stifle opposition. Political opponents had reasonable space to operate from, without undue disturbance from state institutions – again this is in comparison with the earlier two regimes.

Chiluba only established the Human Rights Commission at the behest of the donors who deplored his governance record. But even then, the Commission did not have the nerve to take on the government over human rights violations. There was a change under Mwanawasa. That the Commission could condemn government for human rights violations showed that it had found its long-lost teeth. The decentralisation of the Commission to the provinces was yet indicative of a desire to take institutions of governance closer to the people. However, the Commission suffered from insufficient funding and logistical tools which affected its execution of functions.

One issue most African governments have been grappling with is congestion in prisons. Zambia is no exception. All the prisons in the country were built to cater for a smaller population. But the prisons currently serve a population far beyond their capacity. For instance, in June 2007 Mwanawasa revealed that a prison meant for one hundred was accommodating 1,000 inmates. Consequently, the problem of congestion in prisons remains at worrisome levels. Although the Human Rights Commission has continuously highlighted the problem and made suggestions to government, little has changed. Apart from staying in unpleasant conditions, it takes years for inmates to have their cases disposed of as the wheels of justice grind at a painfully slow speed.

The death penalty has always been a contentious issue in many countries. Constitutions guarantee the right to life as a fundamental human right. But the same constitutions take away the right by imposing the death penalty for certain offences. Although Zambia's Constitution provides for the death penalty and mandates the President to be the 'hangman', Mwanawasa refused to sign any death warrant. The only way out of this quagmire was to commute death sentences to life imprisonments or offer pardon on occasions such as Africa Freedom Day and Independence Day as had been the custom. At the time of writing, the draft constitution also retained the death penalty.

'They are imperialist agencies'
The return to a multi-party democracy gave birth to a vibrant civil society that has grown over the years in both numbers of organisations and militancy. Civil

society organisations have claimed their stake in the affairs of the nation and have provided checks and balances. Chiluba was a product of civil society, having come from trade union circles, but he was very intolerant of civic groups. In 1998 his government initiated a process of creating legislation to regulate NGOs. He left office without enacting that law, but it did not change his attitude towards civil society. With a tone of a self-proclaimed Pan Africanist, he always dismissed civil society as agents of foreign powers sponsored to create chaos in the country.

As with Chiluba, Mwanawasa's view of civil society was one of mistrust. He remained intolerant of vocal civic groups, insisting they were merely political parties disguised as NGOs[1]. He, like Chiluba, believed they were agents of foreign interests, out to destabilise the government. The decision to bring NGO legislation with contentious provisions was one way of curtailing the freedoms of a group of organisations considered nosey. I remember attending a civil society workshop in Lusaka where Justice Minister George Kunda bluntly stated that the administration was determined to regulate NGOs because, he alleged, some of them could be couriers for funding terrorists and homosexuals. Although Mwanawasa did not enact that into law, he remained contemptuous of civil society. It is important to mention that only those NGOs that took on the administration over governance issues were under attack and were the ones targeted under the NGO law which only came to pass under Mwanawasa's successor.

In an attempt to create a 'twin-face' of civil society, the MMD had over the years sponsored certain individuals to pose as *bonafide* NGO leaders. This group of 'civil society' were always in support of the government and against the political opposition. Mwaanga, the MMD's most celebrated political operative, was behind their creation. He even claimed that "many African governments" sponsor NGOs for the purpose of supplying information to the party in power.

---

1   In this chapter , the words 'NGOs' and 'civil society' have been used interchangeably

'We are still consulting'

A government is judged on many fronts. One of them is how it deals with the media. While the traditional role of the media is to inform, entertain and educate, they have another role of providing checks and balances to government, hence contributing to the raising of governance standards. Mwanawasa could have done more to improve the media environment. However, the media were well aware that, like other freedoms, this would not happen easily. As Martin Luther King Jr. once said, "freedom is never voluntarily given by the oppressor, it must be demanded by the oppressed." So the media pushed for various laws aimed at improving the environment in which they operated.

Government passed the Independent Broadcasting Authority (IBA) Act and the Zambia National Broadcasting Corporation (ZNBC) Act of 2002. But it is important to state that these two laws were coming on the back of sustained pressure from media organisations. The media, with the support of some media friendly legislators, came up with the three bills including the Freedom of Information Bill. Realising they were beaten at their own game, the government hastily assembled their own version which they presented to Parliament. The shame attached to these laws was that seven years after they were passed, they never saw the light of implementation. The ZNBC Act was only selectively applied with the collection of a television licence fee by the State broadcaster.

The interpretation of the IBA Act was the subject of a protracted legal battle between media bodies and the government which went up to the Supreme Court, with the government finally prevailing. The contention was on the word 'recommend'. The question was whether the Minister of Information and Broadcasting Services was obliged to accept without question the names of people recommended to sit on the IBA Board. After the court battle, the government went to sleep over the implementation of the law, preferring to make empty promises. Not having laws to govern certain operations is bad enough, but having laws that are not implemented is not helpful either.

Another law that should have been implemented was the Freedom of

Information Act. At the time of writing, it had been ten years after the government withdrew the Bill from Parliament. The media had made their case plain. Firstly, that the law was not only for journalists but a vital tool for governance. Secondly, that if the government intended to fight corruption, that law was a necessity. Although the media had over the years contributed to the fight against corruption, they had done so in a difficult climate. On one hand, government displayed a missionary zeal to rout graft but, on the other, it was not willing to pass supportive legislation. The contradiction could not be more glaring. Trips were made to the UK, Kenya and South Africa, among other countries, to consult on the Freedom of Information Bill. But its enactment remained a subject of endless promises. Excuses that the government was "still consulting over the matter" became monotonous. The failure to enact this law despite all the work done on it was a huge minus.

Mwanawasa's record on the media was far from being tyrannical, but there were cases where irrationality prevailed over reason. In 2002, three journalists were arrested for allegedly defaming him. Despite the offence being a bailable one, the journalists languished in prison for a month at the pleasure of the State. The merits or demerits of the case aside, the events of the case gave the impression that if you were up against the Head of State your case was considered differently. This defamation case demonstrates that Mwanawasa, like Chiluba, could resort to colonial era media restrictions to punish journalists whenever he felt offended, despite campaigns by media rights activists for him to repeal such draconian laws.

Dispatching the prosecutor
Mwanawasa had cultivated a reputation of a respecter of the rule of law. However, there were times he acted contrary to that reputation and engaged in complete lawlessness. As a lawyer, he could have done better. But perhaps it is a lesson and a reminder that sometimes, there can be a gulf between reputation and reality.

Take the case of the Director of Public Prosecutions (DPP), for instance. In January 2004 Mwanawasa received reports that DPP Mukelabai Mukelabai had secretly met with the indicted former intelligence chief Xavier Chungu in the southern resort city of Livingstone. Mwanawasa said the reports were yet to be confirmed. Mukelabai did admit he was in Livingstone on holiday with his daughters, but said he never met Chungu. The damage had been done and questions were already being asked what the chief prosecutor was supposedly doing meeting with a key suspect.

Acting on hearsay, Mwanawasa suspended Mukelabai and sent him on forced leave. That act was illegal and a lawyer of Mwanawasa's pedigree ought to have known what the law stated.

Article 58 (3) of the Constitution stated:

> If the President considers that the question of removing a person holding the office of Director of Public Prosecutions from office ought to be investigated, then:
>
> (a) He shall appoint a tribunal which shall consist of a Chairman and not less than two other members, who hold or have held high judicial office;
>
> (b) The tribunal shall inquire into the matter and report on the facts thereof to the President and advise the President whether the person holding the office of Director of Public Prosecutions ought to be removed from office under this Article for incompetence or inability or for misbehaviour.

Some institutions and individuals that had appointed themselves as underwriters of Mwanawasa's anti-corruption crusade jumped on the bandwagon and denounced Mukelabai. This group was among the renowned worshippers of the Task Force. So their real interest was not the integrity of the DPP's office, but elevating the Task Force by flaying Mukelabai. They mounted a vicious campaign for him to resign, but he refused, seemingly not wanting to legitimise illegality. The Law Association of Zambia backed him.

Mwanawasa then chose to do the right thing by appointing a Tribunal to probe Mukelabai. High Court judge Esau Chulu chaired the Tribunal and was assisted by two other judges, Charles Kajimanga and Philip Musonda.

After hearing from twenty witnesses, the Tribunal cleared Mukelabai and concluded that the allegation of misbehaviour which Mwanawasa had made could not be established. The Tribunal further stated that public confidence in the DPP had waned as a result of the allegations against him. Mukelabai was retired with full benefits. Those who had bayed for his blood didn't even have the moral decency to admit they were wrong. They simply kept quiet and pretended nothing had happened. Those who hold the view that Mukelabai was victimised and sent to his early grave are within their right.

The loss of public confidence in the DPP could not have arisen had Mwanawasa not chosen to act based on what he himself had said were unconfirmed reports. But why would a President who had all the machinery at his disposal to establish facts rely on rumours? Was he misled by people who had other interests?

Mwanawasa had his fair share of promoting good governance and the rule of law. But in a number of instances he rocked his own boat.

CHAPTER TEN

STRUGGLE FOR THE DOCUMENT

"A Constitution is not the act of a government, but of a people constituting a government, and a government without a Constitution is a power without right." – **Thomas Paine (1737-1809), English-American writer and activist.**

AT THE TIME Mwanawasa assumed and vacated office, Zambia had had four Constitutions. The first one was inherited from the colonialists. In 1972 the Constitution was changed to create the one party state. Opposition political parties were outlawed and UNIP became the only political party allowed to exist. Matthias Mainza Chona, an eminent British-trained lawyer and politician who also served twice as Prime Minister, chaired the 1972 Constitution Review Commission (CRC).

In response to growing demands for the country to revert to multi-party politics, which demands UNIP could no longer ignore, the Constitution was altered in 1991 to accommodate those demands. The 1991 CRC was headed by Professor Patrick Mphanza Mvunga, another prominent lawyer and academician. Mvunga also served as Solicitor General and Permanent Secretary in the then Ministry of Legal Affairs (now Ministry of Justice). The 1991 CRC explored many other issues but the most outstanding was the expunging of Article 4 to provide for political plurality and consequently the 1991 multi-party elections.

Article 4 (1) of the 1972 Constitution stated that, "There shall be one and only one political party or organisation in Zambia, namely, the United National Independence Party, (in this Constitution referred to as "The Party")." The removal of that article unbanned political organisations in the country and effectively brought to an end UNIP's supremacy on the political scene. Zambia once again returned to multi-party political activity after seventeen years of 'the Party and its Government'.

Zambia's constitutional instability is a subject scholars have pondered upon at length. Why such an important document has been the subject of so many reviews and a highly contested affair has itself generated a lot of debate, especially given examples where the constitution of countries such as the United States of America has been in place for over two hundred years without any major controversies. Closer to Zambia, South Africa, a late entrant into the democratic sphere, quickly got its act together and within two years promulgated a constitution that has become a reference point for many in Africa.

Mbao (2007) notes that "…throughout the history of constitutional reform in Zambia, there has often been tension between the need to encourage consensus and popular involvement on the one hand and the need to ensure that government's authority is not undermined on the other hand."

Matibini (2007) argues that:

The major reason for constitutional instability in Zambia is that since the attainment of political independence the successive constitutions have lacked legitimacy and moral authority. The question of legitimacy of the constitution is concerned with how to make a constitution command the loyalty and confidence of the people. In order for a constitution to command the loyalty and confidence of the people, the constitution must be understood and acceptable to the people. And to achieve this understanding and acceptance a constitution needs to be put through a process of popularization with a view to generating public interest in it and an attitude that everybody has a stake in it.

The summary of the above is that constitution-making processes that omit the feelings and desires of the people cannot be expected to serve the people. It is also true that where citizens have demanded a greater involvement in the affairs of the nation via the Constitution, politicians have slyly fended off such demands and retained wide-ranging powers to determine the destiny of the country, much to the exclusion of the led.

This is evidenced by the fact that all along constitution-making has been dominated by the Executive. While the people have indeed been given an opportunity to say what type of Constitution they desire, this does not mean their will has prevailed over the narrow interests of politicians. The ruling elites have always retained the power to decide what to accept and what not to. Over time, politicians have imposed themselves as deciders of what is good for the people. This is not only patronising but also brings into question just whose interests are being served.

The writers of the Mung'omba Constitution Review Commission Report could not have put it any better when they noted, inter alia, that "A constitution is not an ordinary piece of legislation. It is the people's sovereign and inalienable right to determine the form of governance for their country by giving to themselves a constitution of their own making."

Given the above and the narrative yet to follow, it can be boldly said that Constitutions made in Zambia have not been a making of the people but a selection of politicians' interests and that is what has essentially created the endless debate on the Constitution. On the one hand, politicians say 'trust us', on the other, the people say 'no, you have failed us before, we can't trust you.'

Condemned by past deceit

The group that beat Kaunda at the election did not need to promise much because the country was ready for change, anyway. They happened to be in the right place at the right time. But to show that they were not just taking advantage of circumstance, Chiluba's MMD came to power carrying a pack of reformist promises, both politically and economically.

Two years into office, Chiluba made an attempt at constitutional reform. In 1993 Legal Affairs Minister Dr Rodger Chongwe appointed a committee of technocrats to draft a new Constitution. Chiluba rejected that route. Instead he appointed John Mupanga Mwanakatwe, a distinguished lawyer and educationist, to head another CRC whose final product Chiluba assented to on 28 May 1996. Those that have followed the debate on constitution-making have always marvelled at the quality of recommendations Mwanakatwe made. Apart from Chiluba rejecting 70% of the recommendations, the 1996 Constitution was controversial in more ways than one as it was aimed at barring Kaunda from contesting that year's presidential election, as well as securing Chiluba's victory.

Kaunda had made what looked like a serious political comeback and was set to contest the general election due that year. But Chiluba, motivated by considerations of political survival, made sure a discriminatory clause was inserted to 'fix' Kaunda. This was a parentage clause that barred people with parents not born in Zambia from standing for the presidency. Kaunda's parents hailed from Malawi. Chiluba did not stop there. He included another clause that barred traditional leaders from participating in politics. That knocked out Senior Chief Inyambo Yeta who was Kaunda's deputy. Although UNIP boycotted the election in protest, in reality they had been eliminated from the race before it even began.

When Chiluba assented to the new Constitution in 1996, the MMD went ballistic, content that they had managed to exclude Kaunda who appeared to have been their most menacing opponent. But this same law nearly caught Chiluba on the wrong foot. His parentage was contested by the opposition after the election as they suspected him of being from neighbouring Zaire, now Democratic Republic of Congo. A man claiming to be Chiluba's father surfaced and insisted that he, Luka Chabala Kafupi, was Chiluba's biological father. Chiluba was accused of disowning 'his father' to evade the parentage clause that he created specifically for Kaunda. Given Kafupi's strong claims and his striking resemblance to Chiluba, it would have been interesting to know what the DNA test result would have shown. But the Supreme Court refused to subject Chiluba to the DNA test demanded by the opposition.

Another provision that Chiluba tinkered with was the Constituent Assembly which Mwanakatwe had recommended as the mode of adopting the new Constitution. He also turned down a provision that would require a winning presidential candidate to amass 50%+1 of the vote despite overwhelming support from the public. Thus, the 1996 Constitution remained a source of conflict for its numerous inconsistencies with a democratic culture.

Writing on the '1991 Constitutional Crisis' in his book *End of Kaunda Era,* Mwanakatwe could not have been more apt about the value of a good constitution when he stated that, "A Constitution works efficaciously when it is widely accepted by the people to whom it gives protection. Therefore, a Constitution which is not widely accepted cannot serve any useful purpose. Often it is not even worth the paper on which it is written."

Instead of being "widely accepted", the 'Chiluba constitution' was a widely rejected and disgraced document and, to borrow further from Mwanakatwe, "not even worth the paper on which it is written". But since for Chiluba and his cohorts political survival was the only motivating factor, they did not care about the wishes of the people, the makers and owners of the Constitution. There were many examples of Chiluba's stubborn refusal to yield to the demands of the people. The issue of the Constitution stands out.

'I commit myself'

A year into office, Mwanawasa initiated another process of constitutional reforms. On 17 April 2003, he appointed a forty one-member CRC chaired by Wila Mung'omba, a lawyer, businessman and banker who had also served as president of the African Development Bank. The product arising from this process would be Zambia's fifth constitution.

Some interest groups, though, had opposed the appointment of another CRC on grounds that the Chona, Mvunga and Mwanakatwe Commissions had already done the work which therefore only needed revisiting and collating into a new Constitution. The Non-Governmental Organisations Coordinating Council (NGOCC), an umbrella body of several NGOs, went to court to challenge the CRC and appointment of the commissioners. They argued that it was illogical for a country facing high unemployment, poverty and HIV and AIDS to spend additional sums of money on a programme that could be avoided. They lost and Mwanawasa went ahead with his plan.

The Mwanawasa Years: An Analysis of his Presidency

In appointing the CRC, Mwanawasa sounded as if he wanted to break with the past. He lamented that the conduct of politicians in the past caused the masses to lose confidence in the government. He bravely and correctly stated that past constitution reviews were done for political expedience. Addressing members of the CRC at State House on 4 May 2003, he delivered a masterpiece of a speech. Having watched Zambian politics for a while, I know that so many speeches lack ownership and are merely delivered because they have to be. But in this one, you are tempted to give Mwanawasa a huge benefit of the doubt that he was speaking from the deepest chamber of his heart and soul. Had he stuck to pronouncements contained therein, his government would have presided over a less acrimonious constitutional reform process. To help put this subject in perspective, the speech is reproduced below in substantial detail:

Recent attempts at constitutional reforms have in fact demonstrated that political survival considerations have been the sole and paramount motivation for these reforms, to the extent of enacting provisions which were not only discriminatory against our citizens, but which were targeted against and or disadvantaged certain individuals usually at the expense of genuine democratic reforms which guaranteed and protected the rights and freedoms of our people.

Naturally, this deceit, this greed and appetite for power, and more power, have polarised the constitutional reform attempts. The Zambian people, and indeed the international community, have come to believe that all other attempts to come at constitutional reforms, including this one, are driven and inspired by the politicians in power, to either entrench themselves or engage in deceit or as a method of creating a political campaign platform for themselves.

Zambians have every right to be cynical about these attempts. Indeed, all of us have every right and reason to feel cynical and cheated, to the point where perhaps we have lost faith in ever producing a people inspired constitution. Sometimes, I am embarrassed and ashamed to find myself as president, in an office, which no longer inspires confidence of our people, I am holding an office, which really has lost the very necessary confidence required to administer our nation effectively. We are constantly judged by the misbehaviour and indiscipline of others. Society no longer trusts us. This is very sad, and an extremely dangerous way of managing a country.

My own profession as a lawyer, has also been drawn into question of reputation; that in spite of a very humble professional background which professes adherence to laws and good order, I too, I am deemed to behave like the other men, who cheated society, who enacted bad laws and who short changed Zambians on the constitution.

It is essentially on this very sad historical background that we find ourselves disagreeing even on a matter which all of us ought to be agreeing. But even when we agree on essentially all the fundamentals, we have still chosen to disagree because we do not trust each other.

But in spite of these disagreements, which are based on mistrust and past experiences, we have nevertheless chosen and decided to go ahead at these constitutional reforms. We do so, not because we seek power, or that we desire to play a game of deceit, or that we mean to cheat.

We do so, because we do not believe in the current constitution as a good basis for political, social and economic emancipation. We do so because, we recognize that the current constitution is not only defective, inadequate and oppressive in many ways, but that it has become altogether suffocating and a source of conflict and confrontation in our land.

With all the good attempts at political harmony and democracy, our constitution fails us. With all the good attempts and intentions at social and economic development, we have been a disaster and continue to remain one of the poorest countries in the world. With all the desires and quests for freedoms and rights for our people, we are still enslaved by our own constitution, and continue to remain in painful bondage.

Yes, we have agreed to make yet another attempt, because we cannot surrender ourselves to past deceit and failure. We have a duty to our nation; to ourselves first, and forever to our posterity. We cannot give up on our nation and on our people, just because some president and his leadership cheated on us. We must accept that we were cheated and deceived, yes. But let us not give up on this account, but rather learn lessons from it, and continue to try.

I am neither disappointed nor angry, about continuously being equated to past failures, not only on the constitution reforms, but on just about everything. It is a terrible legacy. But please do understand, when you can, that like all Zambians, I too am a victim of deceit and dishonesty displayed in previous constitutional reviews, and of past political, social, economic malaise.

My duty and responsibility, I feel, is to restore this credibility and trust, both in the presidency and in the administration of government. I know the difficulties in fighting corruption and lawlessness, I know the difficulties in turning around our economy, and I know the difficulties in inspiring confidence in the constitution reform process. I have even come to know the dangers of implementing good governance in our country. But there cannot either be fear or surrender.

Mr. Chairperson, members of the commission, fellow countrymen and women, I want you to know and to assure you that I have no personal interest to serve in these constitution reforms, neither do I desire to remain president for any longer than necessary. This is not Levy Mwanawasa's constitution, but the people's constitution, and I seek not that my personal views or preferences override the views or preferences of the people. I only desire that working together with all Zambians, I leave a constitution, which shall stand the test of time. I do not seek favour from you Members of the Commission. I only ask that you grant that favour to our people by being bold and patriotic enough to recommend a constitution, which meets their desires and aspirations, which will spur democracy and national development.

Struggle for the Document

The appointment of the constitution review commissioners is a legal and constitutional requirement in the constitutional review process and which, as president, I am obliged to perform. In doing so, dear commissioners, and in accepting this responsibility, please be reminded that your allegiance, loyalty and duty, is not to the appointing authority, but to the people of Zambia, who shall come to you requesting you to listen and capture their views, their wishes and aspirations. From now on, the people of Zambia are your masters, and you shall do what they say; indeed what reflects their wishes and aspirations.

On my part, and indeed on the part of my government, we shall not do anything, which obstructs or undermines the work of the commission, or anything, which undermines the objective of completely achieving the will and the aspirations of our people.

In this regard, I pledge and do hereby commit myself and my government except as impeded by law or by lack of resources to uphold the will and aspirations of our people through their submission to the constitution review commission and to implement the recommendations of the constitution review commission as representing the broadest views of our people.

Let it not be historically registered that Zambia failed to attain a people desired constitution because Levy Mwanawasa as president, and his government subverted the work of the Constitution Review Commission. Instead and at most let it be said that failure was perhaps due to the Commission itself or collectively due to all the Zambians. These are the burdens we now carry. We cannot let the Zambian people down again.

It is very clear that a great number of our people would prefer that the mode of adoption of the next Constitution should be through a constituent assembly. I have said many a time that I too prefer the adoption of the constitution through a constituent assembly. I do not know what else I should say on the constituent assembly more than what I have said before!

> *I have therefore prepared for each of you a copy of my statement, which I read on both radio and television when I announced the establishment of the Commission. My honourable cabinet colleagues present with me will answer any questions, which arise, from that statement or any aspect of this matter in that statement. I have outlined a number of legal, social and economic hurdles, which I perceive as standing in the way to achieving a smooth access to that target.*
>
> *If the commission through submissions is able to get around these difficulties, then let the Commission so indicate to government. It is therefore necessary, that as commissioners, and in addition to receiving submissions under the outlined terms of reference, you attempt to also explore the methods and means of achieving these recommendations. As your President, I feel that it is my duty to bring any difficulties I perceive to your attention and to ask that together we bear the moral duty or commitment to find a solution or to prove that these perceived hurdles are non-existent.*

With that well-crafted dispatching lecture, the CRC went around the country, collected the people's views and produced an Interim Report and Draft Constitution which were delivered on 29 June 2005 to Mwanawasa and the public simultaneously. The simultaneous release of the documents was facilitated by an amendment to Section 5 of the Inquiries Act. Before that, the Draft Constitution would be handed to the President, who together with his Cabinet, would choose what they wanted and reject what they did not. This choice was contained in a document called a white paper. This was what Chiluba and his group did.

In *Teacher, Politician, Lawyer: My Autobiography,* Mwanakatwe recollects how he felt like a pupil being chastised by a headmaster when Chiluba blasted him for the simultaneous release of the Draft Constitution and Report. Ideally, Chiluba would have wanted to have the first look, and by extension, an opportunity to manipulate the document. So Chiluba's annoyance with

Struggle for the Document

Mwanakatwe had nothing to do with anything unlawful Mwanakatwe had done, but everything with Chiluba's intentions to 'doctor' the final outcome.

In the case of the Mung'omba Draft, six months were given for public comments after which the Final Draft was handed to government and to the public simultaneously on 31 December 2005. The CRC had fulfilled their mandate as given to them by Mwanawasa. Now here began the manoeuvres.

Not your road map, but ours
Government not only vigorously opposed the key recommendations in the final draft but also rejected outright the document as "defective." The retention in the Final Draft of most of the recommendations cheered civil society and opposition parties as it reflected the wishes of the people and demonstrated that the CRC resisted any attempts by the Executive to manipulate the outcome. But the government was not amused. Interestingly, the same recommendations that Chiluba and his group had rejected in 1996 like adopting the Constitution through a Constituent Assembly, a winning presidential candidate amassing 50%+1 of the vote, having an elected Vice President, were the same provisions that Mwanawasa's government also rejected, although in Mwanawasa's case the provisions remained in the document, as opposed to Chiluba who expunged them. That Zambians had repeatedly made these submissions was a clear desire that they wanted them contained in their Constitution. But politicians, who were merely serving at the pleasure of the voters, were in the forefront denying the people their choice. Not even Mwanawasa who spoke so well about past failures could get it right. It has since become clear that politicians are never quite comfortable when it comes to accountability and when the people demand a broader participation in administering national affairs.

Before the CRC finished its work, Mwanawasa had accused some stakeholders, particularly civil society and the opposition, of predetermining the process. But even after the CRC presented to him what *the people* had said, his government could not accelerate the pace. It wandered from claiming logistical and financial hurdles to the need not to rush the process. Mwanawasa had given the CRC thirty one detailed Terms of References. The timeframe for producing a new Constitution was not included. Perhaps that was calculated.

Long before Mwanawasa initiated the process, civil society presented itself as an amalgamated force under the Oasis Forum. It was formed in 2001 at a meeting held at the Oasis Restaurant in the Lusaka showgrounds. The meeting was held at the height of Chiluba's attempt to have a third term. A loose alliance of Church groups, the Law Association of Zambia and several NGOs robustly fought Chiluba until he backed off. It then established itself as an alternative voice taking on government on various governance issues, with the push for a new Constitution being its flagship activity.

Mwanawasa and civil society regularly clashed over several governance issues, but the fight over the Constitution stood out. He rejected opposition and civil society demands that the new document be ready before the 2006 election, insisting it could not be rushed for the sake of elections. He found solace in the past record, saying the reason the country had failed to have a durable Constitution that encompassed majority interests was that it was rushed to serve the political interests of the time.

Realising Mwanawasa would not succumb, the counter forces tried another route they hoped would serve as a consolation for his refusal to hasten the process. On two occasions ahead of the election, the Oasis Forum and the opposition attempted to amend election-related legislation, specifically the 50%+1 threshold. Their argument was that a President elected with that threshold went into office with reasonable legitimacy.

Government dismissed the proposed amendments as "piecemeal." In any case, it argued, there was no need for duplication because the Draft Constitution contained the same provision. The counter argument from civil society and opposition was that while the government had refused to enact a new Constitution before the election, certain provisions could be made as a compromise.

Mwanawasa flatly refused. Instead, he quickly rushed through Parliament, and enacted, a new Electoral Act which scandalously omitted several key recommendations made by the Electoral Reforms Technical Committee, a body he had appointed in August 2003 to look into election legislation. The country went to the polls on yet another contentious piece of legislation. At this stage, the need to win an election once again threw politicians into acting for the advancement of their own political interests.

The refusal by government to allow the "piecemeal" amendments was interesting. The 50%+1 was a hotly contested issue. Although they were justified in arguing that the provision was already in the Draft Constitution, they merely used that as an alibi. Their real fear was that they would not amass that threshold at the general election and, as it turned out, they did not.

Gould (2007) notes as follows:

Having squeaked through on a (highly contested) 29 percent plurality in 2001, Mwanawasa was understandably uneasy about his chances for re-election in 2006 under such a provision [the 50%+1]. Through filibustering and political manipulation, MMD stalled constitutional reforms with the result that the 2006 elections were held under the simple majority clause introduced by Chiluba in 1996. From the MMD's perspective this was a prudent tactical move. It is anybody's guess how Mwanawasa would have fared against Sata had the elections gone into a second round.

Mwanawasa won the election with 42%, against Sata's 29%. It is clear where the contest would have ended had the polls been held under the proposed revised legislation which the MMD vigorously shot down. A second round of voting would have provided a real test for both contestants.

Elections passed and the stalemate over the Constitution continued with government and other interest groups at variance. While the latter insisted the Constitution could be ready in a short time, Mwanawasa argued that he would not engage in "short cuts". The wrangling and rambling continued. The fact that the next step in the process lay with the Executive meant it would take its own pace.

137

Having intelligently diagnosed the ills in past attempts at constitutional reform, Mwanawasa should have driven the process in a manner reflective of his understanding. He should have avoided practices that would erode public confidence even further. Unfortunately, as the process went on, Mwanawasa drifted and headed for the same ditch into which other politicians had fallen. He went into ways that soon began to undermine the people's confidence.

In the speech above, Mwanawasa had openly declared his support for a Constituent Assembly as the mode of adopting the new constitution. He said, "I have said many a time that I too prefer the adoption of the constitution through a Constituent Assembly. I do not know what else I should say on the Constituent Assembly more than what I have said before!"

The government, through the Fifth National Development Plan (FNDP), had committed itself to the enactment of the new constitution via a Constituent Assembly. Under an elaborate chapter on Governance, the FNDP stated that: "The Government shall facilitate the process that shall usher in a new Republican Constitution that shall be adopted during the FNDP period [2006-2010] by the Constituent Assembly."

In its submissions to the CRC on 24 September 2004, the MMD had stated that, "...If the people of Zambia decide on the mode of adoption through the Constituent Assembly, then the MMD is of the view that Government should implement that decision as the will of the people."

But despite all this support for the Constituent Assembly, Mwanawasa changed and became its famed opponent. He stunned the nation by announcing that come the referendum he would vote against the Constituent Assembly. While he was entitled to such a democratic right, he should not have, in the first place, pulled the wool over the people's eyes into believing him over something he had no intention of respecting. Why he had consistently declared support for a Constituent Assembly only to oppose it later is puzzling. With that position taken, nothing different could be expected from his circle. They, too, publicly adopted a position that obstinately defied the people's will.

Civil society developed an alternative road map including the holding of a Constituent Assembly to enact the new constitution. They even offered to mobilise funds for that purpose. But Mwanawasa rejected their road map, insisting it was defective. Instead he charted a road map that meant asking Zambians whether or not they wanted a Constituent Assembly to adopt the Constitution. But that question had already been resolved when the people submitted to the Mung'omba CRC. Among the Terms of Reference Mwanawasa had given the CRC was to recommend the mode of adopting the new Constitution. The CRC recommended the Constituent Assembly based on the people's submissions. Therefore, calling for a referendum to ask Zambians the very same question they had already answered was condemned as a waste of time and money. It was surprising that an administration that had earlier pleaded lack of finances could now employ a process that would gobble even more money. However, just when civil society launched a campaign against the proposed referendum in June 2007, Mwanawasa saw the writing on the wall. He back-pedalled.

Political events in Africa have a way of either repeating themselves, or being so similar that the result is almost always predictable. For instance, in November 2005 Kenyan President, Mwai Kibaki suffered a humiliating defeat in a referendum. The cause was no different from the route Mwanawasa had initiated. When campaigning for the 2002 general election, Kibaki had promised to deliver a new Constitution within one hundred days of taking office. When it came three years later, it was in a form the people had rejected. But Kibaki refused to listen to what the people wanted and, despite his allies advising him, he went ahead with the condemned draft. Politicians who never want to hearken to the people's voice do, in many, cases bring about their own downfall. When the referendum came, the people voted a massive 'NO'. Kibaki's loss led to a collapse of his government, as his own Cabinet ministers had led the opposition to the draft and later broke away to form their own parties. The loss was also a huge show of no confidence in Kibaki, which saw his rating take a deep dip. In other countries, this would be enough reason to step down. But this is rarely seen amongst African politicians.

Civil society had warned Mwanawasa that if he called a referendum and lost, he should have also been prepared to resign, as he would have lost legitimacy. Thus losing a referendum carried with it grave political consequences, which it is doubtful Mwanawasa was prepared to face. It is difficult to figure out why Mwanawasa attempted to have a referendum and where he got the confidence that he could win it. But it's also possible that he was merely testing public opinion and he got the result, not only more quickly, but also with a force he may not have anticipated. He changed course.

Bind us together

By 2007, four years after the process had begun, there was no end to the government's manoeuvres. The process had already taken more twists and turns than a detective novel. Civil society had mounted a vigorous effort at defending what they regarded to be in the public interest. Government, on the other hand, believed that as the elected, they carried the people's mandate and were therefore right in driving the process in the manner they did. Despite several meetings between civil society and Mwanawasa, they could not agree on the way forward, with the two parties constantly trading accusations and mistrust.

Mwanawasa rejected the view that civil society was speaking for the people. He habitually attacked civil society, claiming they had no part in political affairs. They were not amused. Civil society had already reminded him that had they not vigorously campaigned to curtail Chiluba's excitement over the third term bid he, would not be President.

In June 2007, the same time civil society had launched a 'No Referendum' campaign, Mwanawasa convened a meeting of political leaders under the auspices of the Zambia Centre for Interparty Dialogue (ZCID). In a rare show of unity, political party leaders held hands and intoned 'Bind us together Lord, bind us together with cords that cannot be broken.'

After the meeting it emerged that they had agreed that the adoption of the Draft Constitution would now take the route of a 'Constitutional Conference'.

In its report, the Mung'omba Commission had, apart from the Constituent Assembly, provided for "any other popular body" to adopt the Constitution. Enter the National Constitutional Conference (NCC). This, too, was another contentious phase.

It is worth noting that all along, although the opposition did make comments on the process, it was mainly civil society that took on government over the matter. But at this stage, the forces in the battle had been realigned. Mwanawasa had managed to enlist opposition parties to support his new plan. The opposition which had previously been supportive of the civil society position went along with Mwanawasa. How they now chose to support him, when they had all along dismissed him as untrustworthy, is part of the shifting sands in politics. Politicians who were initially at loggerheads were now presenting themselves as 'constitution saviours'! Not that they should not have worked together. But to have done so in a manner which alienated other key stakeholders, such as civil society, was turning constitution-making into a preserve of colluding politicians.

Although the opposition Patriotic Front attended the ZCID meeting, it later pulled out and sided with civil society. Political convictions are never permanent, or so it seems. In December 2005, when the UPND and other opposition parties joined the Oasis Forum in demonstrating over a new Constitution, Michael Sata refused to join. Political parties and NGOs had nothing in common, he said. But there he was two years later siding with the NGOs.

Zambian politicians are collectively guilty for the mess the country has found itself in over this matter. Some of the most vocal, those who seek to offer solutions, were part of the crop that Chiluba used in committing fraud over the writing of a new Constitution. For instance, when civil society picketed Parliament in protest against the 1996 Constitution, one leader of the MMD who is now an opposition leader, dismissed them as "anarchists bent on fanning chaos that would frighten away investors." Other MMD members danced and celebrated when Chiluba assented to it. Today, they all know what a good Constitution reads like when they failed to bequeath one to the people of Zambia or at least failed to oppose Chiluba in designing a defective one.

Much as politicians take comfort in 'collective responsibility', logic demands that you cannot align yourself with something you do not agree with and still be at peace with yourself. It is not a sin in politics to leave because your personal view contradicts that of others, no matter their number. Those who did not agree with Chiluba over his mishandling of the Constitution resigned in protest. Those who remained did so with a clear conscious for which they must be unsympathetically judged.

Back to Mwanawasa. With some of the opposition parties on his side, he dashed to Parliament and enacted the National Constitutional Conference (NCC) Act. The Constituent Assembly was now out of the vocabulary and in came the NCC. The NCC debated and allegedly refined the Mung'omba Draft Constitution. But by all indications, it appeared this would be another sham of an undertaking.

Like any other social study, law and politics are not an exact science. However, there is a world of difference between holding diverse opinions and failing to keep promises. This chapter has attempted to lean more on the promises Mwanawasa made regarding constitutional reforms, how he had asked Zambians to trust him, how he had promised to be different and how he finally veered from the initial path and took a meandering route uncharacteristic of his pledge. Kofi Annan once said "The promises that matter are the promises that are kept." By consistently shifting positions on things he had himself committed to, Mwanawasa had unwittingly surrendered himself to, in his own language, "past deceit."

Given all the above, it can be stated that Mwanawasa and his government were embarrassingly contradictory on constitutional reforms. Going by the passion with which he spoke when he initiated the process and his promises elsewhere that the new Constitution would be ready "as soon as possible", he betrayed his own conscience and irredeemably missed the ship sailing to a constitutional legacy. It's understood that legal reform is not a nine days' wonder. But if years characterised by broken promises are what make up "as soon as possible," then the inventors of the English language could be forgiven for not foreseeing the ambiguity that phrase would cause and how some people would stretch it to embellished lengths.

According to Mulongoti, one of Mwanawasa's failures was that "he could not leave Zambia with a new Constitution. That was the biggest weakness. He started well but he could not crystallise it in the end."

Started well indeed. Having originally stated his intentions on constitutional reforms, Mwanawasa could have crowned it all by delivering on his promise in time and without despising the will of the people. He would have been remembered for that. But he missed it.

However, Mwanawasa deserves credit for moving the process of constitution-making beyond the Executive and the Legislature. It was the first time in Zambia's history that the route of making a constitution had included another body other than the two. But the true measure of this would be judged by the final product which remained elusive at the time of writing.

CHAPTER ELEVEN

SEARCHING FOR THE GOOD LIFE

"Economic growth without social progress lets the great majority of people remain in poverty, while a privileged few reap the benefits of rising abundance." **- John F. Kennedy (1917-1963), 35th President of the USA, 1961 -1963.**

ECONOMIC COMMENTATORS, HISTORIANS and other observers of developments in Zambia remain nostalgic about the state of the economy at independence. They constantly refer to Zambia's economy having been at par with South Korea, and better than Malaysia and Singapore, whose meteoric rise from the economic doldrums has been dubbed 'the Asian miracle.' With vast copper reserves and a zealous crop of nationalists eager to deliver to the people the fruits of hard won independence, Zambia, it is said, represented Africa's best hope.

In an unpublished paper, Di John recollects as follows:

In the 1960s Zambia was a middle-income country believed to have considerable growth potential. In the mid-1960s, no place was emerging faster than Zambia, the newly independent nation that was previously part of a wider colonial federation under British rule. From being a purely agricultural territory at the time of takeover by British mining interests in the 1890s, the modern state of Zambia had by 1969 arrived as the most urbanised country in Africa. Zambia had scores of cities with over 100,000 inhabitants and these cities contained 40 percent of the population. Mineworkers in the leading sector, copper, were among the best paid workers in all of Africa. Copper dominated the economy at independence, and would do so for thirty years despite attempts through government planning and later 'market forces' to diversify.

But much as those romantic memories linger, the fact is that the tables turned. Discussing Zambia's economic booms and busts over the years requires a book of its own. Under this chapter we will restrict ourselves to the subject at hand.

When Kaunda and his colleagues took over the country from the colonialists, the task of nation building before them was immense. They had to shape a country in which all would have a sense of belonging; they had to build a national culture with which to rally everyone towards development. Having come from a background where inequality was the order of the day, where the life of the Zambian was less valued, where certain amenities were only the preserve of a few, the liberators had to work towards making the country a place where all felt valued. The most tangible good that the post-colonial government came up with was infrastructure. In fact, most of the infrastructure – roads, airports, schools, hospitals, bridges, government offices, etc. - that Zambia has relied on over the years was built by the post-independence government.

In its quest to develop the country, Kaunda's administration is said to have worked at an amazing pace. Today when you ask any leader of that generation how they managed to do so much, they will tell you they were driven by servanthood. However, even liberators get it wrong. Despite having done so much in the immediate years after independence, a combination of external factors, wrong policies and bad governance made the country regress economically. So much was the economic damage that when an opportunity arose to change government, Zambians did not hesitate to vote out Kaunda and his fellow freedom fighters. Yes, they had done much for which the country should remain eternally grateful, but they had not only overstayed but had also taken the country on an abysmal path economically.

Anglo pack their bags
When the MMD took over in 1991 the economy was so bad that Chiluba simply said he had inherited a collapsed economy. Having ridden on the

promise of a market economy, Chiluba soon began to liberalise the economy and succeeded in moving the economy into private sector hands, but that was not without problems. The inefficiency of the parastatal sector soon came to light as the new government was not in the socialist habit of subsidising non-performing state-owned firms. Either the firms had over employed, or they were just bankrupt, or both. The investors who bought the former parastatals under the ambitious privatisation drive retained only part of the workforce, while those that were liquidated offloaded all the workers onto the streets. There were mass job losses.

As in Chiluba's case, when Mwanawasa took over, he said he inherited an economy that was on its "total knees." Thus both Chiluba and Mwanawasa blamed the past; I am not sure if Kaunda also blamed the British. The blame game aside, each of them had different economic circumstances when they assumed and left office and they all had a vast array of opportunities to build and improve upon what they found. Leaders are judged for what they do, not what they found. No matter how pathetic a record bequeathed, a leader who consistently blames the past for his failure to deliver is merely seen as an incompetent who uses the past to hide his own inefficiencies.

There were no major policy shifts expected. Mwanawasa was part of the MMD that preached a free market economy in the 1990s and there had been no departure from that message. The only changes were the team captain and the way of doing business. Mwanawasa initiated several developments on the economic front for which he must be credited. While some were of his own making, it is also true that some of the achievements he scored had their roots in the previous administration. For instance, the process of seeking a debt write off from international creditors was started by Chiluba.

Mwanawasa walked into numerous economic challenges, from mounting internal and external debts, massive unemployment, to high inflation and interest rates. Zambia's external debt of over US$7 billion was strangling the economy. However, the immediate crisis he faced within days of takeover was the pull-out of Anglo American Plc from the mining sector. Anglo was the major shareholder in Konkola Copper Mines (KCM), which at the time was the country's biggest mine. About 11,000 jobs at the mine and in other support industries were on the line. At that time you could not talk of Zambia's economy without a reference to the crisis at KCM. That was how serious the matter was. How Mwanawasa's team managed the crisis and ensured that KCM did not close is something even natural sceptics would wish to admire. But the same cannot be said of his government's decision to sell the mine at a ridiculously giveaway price of US$25 million.

After dealing with the crisis at KCM, the huge external debt was the daunting task ahead. To have the debt written off, Zambia underwent austerity from the International Monetary Fund (IMF) and the World Bank. This included freezing civil service wages and spending within limits prescribed by the two institutions. The outcry from the masses could not have been louder and government was criticised for adhering to conditions that were hurting the people.

Mwanawasa's hard line Finance Minister, Ng'andu Magande, put his head on the chopping block. His bold and blunt approach was taken for arrogance. As the main face on economic affairs, he bore the criticism of Mwanawasa's economic policies.

Civil society, galvanised under the 'Jubilee Movement', did a remarkable job of undertaking an aggressive international roadshow campaigning for debt cancellation. The joint civil society and government campaign paid off in April 2005 when creditors announced that Zambia had reached the 'completion point' of the Highly Indebted Poor Countries (HIPC) initiative – never mind the demeaning categorisation. The debt reduced from US$7.2 billion to around US$500 million, a highlight of Mwanawasa's first term which he trumpeted in campaigning for re-election.

Zambia witnessed an upswing in investment and its international profile. Mwanawasa took interest in attending forums that would enhance the country's economic fortunes. His ability to address business communities around the world and speak passionately on the country's economic potential was reassuring. "We want to see the colour of your money," he told an investors' meeting in the US. His interest in more investment than aid showed he understood the long-term benefits of setting the country on a path to self-actualisation. He laid strong emphasis on missions abroad not only to exist as a diplomatic imperative but also to be marketers of the country.

A government that has no plan has no business in governing a country. Kaunda presided over four development plans. But whether the plans came to fruition is another subject altogether. Chiluba dissolved the National Commission for Development Planning into the Ministry of Finance, but did not have a development plan in his decade.

Mwanawasa initiated the Transitional National Development Plan, which ran from 2003-2005. In collaboration with various stakeholders, government designed the Fifth National Development Plan (FNDP) for the period 2006-2010. The FNDP, then projected to gobble K62.6 billion, was anchored on "broad based wealth and job creation through citizenry participation and technological advancement." Alongside the FNDP was the 'Vision 2030' whose major thrust was to turn Zambia into "a prosperous middle income nation by 2030."

The two documents, arising from the Poverty Reduction Strategy Paper (PRSP 2002-2005) and the TNDP (2003-2005), were of great import as even donors (or cooperating partners, as they are courteously referred to in government corridors) were to channel their aid in the context of the development plan. The development by donors of the Joint Assistance Strategy for Zambia (JASZ) was in response to the FNDP. While donors agreed that the FNDP provided an "acceptable basis" for aligning their support, they pointed out the numerous challenges the country would have to address across sectors if targets contained in the FNDP were to be achieved. The JASZ went into details of what Zambia's problems were and what needed to be done to solve them. Suffice to say that much of what the JASZ expounded was not new; the challenges mentioned had been known to hinder development for a long time. Although bold ambitions elaborately laid out in documents are nothing if not implemented, the FNDP, as a development blueprint, was at least a sign that the government had plans and targets and knew precisely which destination they were aiming for.

The economy made noticeable gains, with continuously recorded positive Gross Domestic Product (GDP). In 2005 it posted 5.1% compared to 5.4% in 2004 before rising to 5.8% in 2006. Several economic sectors showed signs of recovery. Agriculture, which had been left for dead, picked up and the country was back in self-sufficiency in food. Agriculture remains the key priority in the growth and poverty reduction programme of the country. Over 60% of the population derives its livelihood from agriculture and resides in rural areas. However, according to the FNDP, in the past, agriculture development did not receive resources commensurate with its status. Government spending on agriculture had been less than 5% of the national budget and less than 1.0% of GDP, far below the 10% of the budget espoused by the Maputo Declaration. This low spending on agriculture-related developments resulted in agricultural support infrastructure being run down, extension service delivery operating at only 40% capacity, and high and repeated livestock disease incidences. The result was low agricultural productivity and high poverty levels, especially in rural areas. The various government and donor supported programmes gave the sector a new face. The decision to place agriculture and infrastructure under 'Targeted Priority Expenditure' in the FNDP would, if implemented, drive growth to higher levels. However, this is not to say everything in the sector remained perfect. Several challenges remained; especially the development of the rural peasant.

Tourism, which had for years been regarded as a social sector, was reclassified as an economic sector and natural endowments were vigorously marketed to tap into the spending power of the world's tourists. How ironic that neighbouring countries with fewer tourist sites were netting more in tourism revenue than Zambia, which boasts breath-taking attractions. In 2005 government launched the 'Visit Zambia' campaign, which was significant in increasing tourist arrivals and in stimulating the involvement of the private sector. However, one of its shortcomings was that it was projected more as an event and less as an ongoing programme. This approach resulted in the marketing of particular segments of the tourism sector such as the 'Northern Circuit' instead of the whole country as a tourism destination.

The curse of the copper spoon

The resurgence of the mining industry under Mwanawasa coincided with the recovery of metal prices on the world market. (If it is true that Anglo left because of low metal prices, then they miscalculated.) Several international mining companies came to exploit the abundant mineral resources. The discovery of other minerals, in addition to copper, aided by increased investment in exploration and machinery, pushed large-scale mining to a higher level. But that investment could not have just dropped like ripe fruit from a tree. It entailed setting the right environment and policies which could attract investors. It also meant running a reasonably credible government that investors would be comfortable dealing with. It was also about investors believing their investment was safe via respect for the rule of law. To that extent, Mwanawasa had delivered.

The Copperbelt, Zambia's industrial heartland, had been left desolate from a combination of factors. Some companies failed to compete under a liberal economic environment and either relocated or closed shop. Others were heavy casualties of botched privatisation deals. Towns such as Ndola and Luanshya, once well known for their industries, were shells of their former selves. However, under Mwanawasa the economic fortunes of the Copperbelt revived with increased investment in various sectors of the economy. That companies were returning to invest was evidence of the improved economic outlook. A new phenomenon was that the Copperbelt was extending to the North-Western Province following the emergence of large-scale mines there. Small and relatively quiet towns such as Solwezi were now home to huge mines.

However, Zambia's wealthiest industry also remains a source of deep frustration for its people. While copper prices hit record levels and mining companies were raking in billions of dollars, this was not reflected in tax revenues in the mineral-producing nation due to tax concessions given to mining companies.

A bit of history is in order here. When Zambia decided to privatise its mines in the 1990s copper prices were low and it was difficult to attract buyers without a sweetener. The former mining conglomerate, the Zambia Consolidated Copper Mines (ZCCM) was sucking as much as US$1 million a day from the treasury to keep the mines running. Finding buyers was therefore urgent. At last, the mines were sold for what critics called "a song" (I apologise to musicians who don't like this phrase) plus overly generous tax concessions of between fifteen and twenty years, ostensibly to cushion buyers from low copper prices. It is common knowledge that the buyers took advantage of the government's extreme anxiety to drive a hard bargain.

At a time when mining firms in other countries paid an average of 3% mineral royalty, in Zambia they got away with a measly 0.6%. When the mines were sold, government signed development agreements with the mine companies. The latter cleverly made sure the agreements were heavily tilted in their favour (whatever happened to Zambia's negotiators?). Renegotiating the agreements presented an uphill battle as they were legally binding; they could not be contradicted by future legislation and any dispute could only be referred to the international arbitration process.

The loss in revenue to Zambia was as graphic as the figures immediately suggest. In 2005 and 2006 copper earnings amounted to US$1.6 billion and US$3.1 billion, respectively, but of these amounts, mining companies paid taxes of only US$26 million in 2005 and US$76 million in 2006. In 2007 mining companies were projected to earn about US$3.5 billion, while their tax contributions were estimated at a paltry US$198 million. Copper prices were high and mining companies were making it big. But they were paying next to nothing in taxes.

Announcing that government would no longer enter into such agreements, Magande expressed his frustration at missing out on the copper boom when he said, "Clearly, this contribution is not consistent with the revenues being made by mining companies and it is a clear inequality in the sharing of revenues from the country's resources and it also demonstrates the lop-sidedness of these agreements."

Belatedly, in 2008 Zambia increased mineral royalty to 3% from 0.6% and introduced the windfall tax. But this was not without grumbling from mining companies that advanced a host of arguments against the increase. They even contemplated going to court. Mining companies are entitled to argue otherwise by repeatedly advancing reasons such as 'mining is an expensive venture', but it is equally true that they have massively ripped off the country, making billions of dollars and polluting the environment, while paying peanuts in taxes. Claims that they are committed to corporate social responsibility, which has seen them build some public infrastructure, amounts to very little when compared to what the country might have done had they paid taxes in the right measure. It has actually been argued that if Zambia had made the most out of its natural resource, there would have been no need to go around begging for aid and being lectured to by junior economists from the IMF.

It was hoped that the new taxes would raise as much as US$400 million in 2008 alone, money that was planned to be invested in the social sector. The increase, though delayed, was hailed as progressive. But too good, too late; the global recession set in and the mining industry was a heavy casualty as metal prices plummeted on the world market. Worse still, by the time the prices rebounded, Mwanawasa's successor had presided over the abolition of the taxes under the grossly misguided view that such taxes were obstructing investment.

The 'greedy' banks

Interest rates are an important indicator of an economy's health. For many years, government's huge borrowing from the market crowded out the private sector. Such borrowing sent interest rates skyrocketing. As government swept all the money from the market to beef up its finance envelope, banks were less inclined to lend to the business sector as they got their profits from lending to government. However, a shift in policy to reduce borrowing resulted in more funds being unlocked from government bonds and securities and made available on the market. Banks now had excess liquidity and reality dawned on them that they would have to look elsewhere as they could no longer solely rely on government stocks. Thus, borrowing, which had been a preserve of a few, due to exorbitant interest rates, was now trickling down to a larger segment of the population. The fact that banks could now advertise loans and compete to lend to the public was evidence that government policy was working. Interest rates, which hovered around 47.4% in 2002, had dropped to 27.1% in 2005. Between 2004 and 2007, the Central Bank reduced Statutory Reserve Ratios twice, which put pressure on commercial banks to reduce interest rates.

Demands, however, continued for interest rates to be lowered further to stimulate economic activity. Appeals from government and the Central Bank for commercial banks to reduce their lending rates even further, in tandem with the changed economic environment, have gone largely unheeded. Yes there has been a reduction, but not enough to enable many people to borrow. In theory, interest rates are supposed to hover around the inflation rate. But banks have their own reasons for not doing so, among them risk factors and the fact that the cost of doing business in Zambia is high. What banks do not say, though, is that the high cost of borrowing is itself a contributor to the high cost of doing business. Thus, even when inflation hit a single digit to as low as 8.2%, interest rates still remained thrice the inflation rate in some cases. Whether that is a pitfall of a free market, or banking greed, or some other economic phenomenon is a debate that cannot be concluded here.

From around K5 to US$1 in 2002, the exchange rate dropped to K2.9 by June 2006, a feat repeated in the middle of 2008. The appreciation of the currency in 2006 got everyone talking – the opposition, the captains of industry and government itself. Several factors accounted for the gains. Increased copper production and exports, aided by high prices on the international market, increased non-traditional exports and the debt write off which meant spending less foreign exchange on debt servicing. But the gain in the currency was a double-edged sword. For importers, it was an opportunity to maximise imports of capital goods and raw materials by using less local currency to buy more foreign currency for their purchases. But exporters were on the losing side and industrialists urged government to act, failure to which the export sector would collapse.

Government argued that much as the gains of the Kwacha had some adverse effect on exporters, the broader picture was one of the entire economy and not just one sector.

For the opposition, the increased strength of the Kwacha was not convincing. They accused government of falsifying the value of the currency to endear themselves to the electorate ahead of the 2006 election. But Mwanawasa refused to have his gains blemished and he bragged, "We have simply performed." Although the exchange rate retreated to slightly higher levels, it largely remained stable as the treasury strove to implement more fiscal measures that would power the local currency.

Renewed donor confidence was a result of several policies implemented. The fight against corruption and improved governance record were some of them. Project and budget support from donors flowed consistently. Important as the donor flows were, many Zambians looked forward to reduced donor dependence and financing development from local resources.

BEE for South Africa, CEE for Zambia

An economy in which citizens are distant or passive participants is a defective one. Government exists solely for the good of its citizens, but no government the world over is expected to deliver food to the homes of its citizens, in the literal sense. However, it is the inescapable duty of every government to create conditions that allow its people to actively participate in the running of the economy and thus generate enough resources to look after themselves.

In previous years, there was a never-ending complaint (it still has not ended, in fact) that government had not done enough to enable its people to become economically empowered. While foreigners had a noticeable stake in the economy, the locals remained disadvantaged. Such scenarios, if left unchecked, have in some countries led to xenophobia against certain groups of people who are perceived to be many classes above the rest. In years gone by, the difference in access to economic opportunities was accounted for in colonialism and its attendant evils. It is true that colonialism had deep-running effects including denying the black man access to a decent means of livelihood. Those who lived through colonialism remember a saying by the colonialist: *'Zambia ena Kawena, Mali ena Katina'*, meaning Zambia is yours, the money is ours. But the colonialists had been gone for many years. If the locals did not have reasonable access to the economy decades after the end of colonialism, the blame lay on the government, and not the long-gone colonisers.

Though many Zambians are said to be industrious, access to finance is one factor highlighted as the most inhibiting. In an economic environment where banks are averse to lending to small businesses on account of high risk, the would-be entrepreneur is locked out despite abounding potential. High risk, though, was not the only reason. Commercial banks were comfortable making their profits from dealing in government securities and, therefore, the trader did not rank high on their list.

In 2005 Mwanawasa appointed a Citizens Economic Empowerment Advisory Committee, tasked with developing a comprehensive empowerment policy to ensure equity and empowerment of Zambian citizens. This produced the Citizens Economic Empowerment (CEE) Act in 2006. The Act was dubbed as a vehicle to promote and stimulate more local participation in the economy because of its inclusiveness, predictability and certainty. The outstanding provision in the Act was the Empowerment Fund aimed at supporting the development of broad-based economic empowerment programmes. Although many businesses complained of encumbrances in accessing the funds, the idea was nonetheless worthwhile.

It is hoped that in later years, the CEE will not attract the criticism its cousin in South Africa has. After the fall of apartheid in 1994, the South

African government introduced the Black Economic Empowerment (BEE), a plan to rescue black citizens from 350 years of economic exploitation, poverty and social degradation. However, the actual benefits accruing to the blacks were said to be elusive and the BEE had been dismissed as a tool for the enrichment of a few politically well-connected black entrepreneurs. That some already well-established white businesses were using blacks as fronts to get business reserved for blacks made the empowerment programme a mockery.

Much as Zambia's economic environment differs fundamentally from South Africa's, the concept of the empowerment programme for both countries remained the same – to prop up disadvantaged locals. Thus the CEE will be judged on how much it delivers on that score.

But where's our share?

Government boasted of macroeconomic successes, but the living conditions of the people remained desperate with the majority of them in poverty, a fact Mwanawasa did not shy away from. By the end of his first term in office, poverty levels had remained high at 68% from 73% when he took over. Mwanawasa frankly admitted he had just "scratched on the surface." In fact, in January 2005 he apologised for failing to reduce poverty. Numerically, there was a growth in GDP, a reduction in inflation and an increase in investment flows in several sectors of the economy. This excites the treasury bureaucrat and some economic commentators who go to great lengths to explain how it was achieved. But all this is meaningless to the ordinary person if there is no change in their lives. The question will always be 'what's in there for the people'? Simply put, an economy that grows only in figures without impacting the lives of the people will always remain an optical illusion and therefore unappreciated.

Ideally, investment should benefit both the investor and the environment in which that investment is domiciled. Any investment exists to maximise shareholder value. But investment that ignores the environment in which it operates is a lopsided one. This imbalance has been a source of frustration in many African countries including Zambia. While the economy continued to attract investors, the actual benefits accruing to the people remained intangible. There were new jobs, but their quality was highly questionable. The poor working conditions in some local and foreign-owned businesses was a source of great worry and brought into question government's interest in the welfare of its people. Examples abound. The country was once treated to news of a government minister crying at the sight of the dehumanising conditions workers were subjected to at the Chinese-owned Collum Coal Mine in Sinazongwe, Southern Province. The workers had no protective clothing. In later years, Chinese managers at this same mine were to shoot eleven of their Zambian workers. In 2005, forty six Zambians died at yet another Chinese-owned firm, manufacturing explosives. Ironically, no Chinese died. No need to beat about the bush. Chinese industries are notorious for poor safety standards.

The desire for higher investment should have been matched by an adequate employment framework that would take into account the needs of labour. Typical of a capitalist system, some employers used the high rate of unemployment to offer mediocre wages and working conditions. Labour unions and the public voiced out over the dehumanising conditions some workers were subjected to. But authorities miserably failed to take strong deterrent measures. The love for investors apparently superseded the need to offer decent working conditions. Labour was at the mercy of capital. By failing to protect workers from exploitation, government appeared as a collaborator in the oppression of its own people. The problem was not the absence of laws, but lack of enforcement. It should be noted that government was not expected to come down hard on investors (local or foreign) when it was also a culprit.

For many years the minimum wage remained at K268. Ridiculous as this was, government did not seem bothered. Investors who were paying slightly above even arrogantly told off their workers that they should be grateful for getting salaries that were above the minimum provision. Perhaps the statement above that 'the government appeared as a collaborator in the oppression of its own people' is an understatement. Government was in fact participating in humiliating its own people. Although the above was not exclusive to Mwanawasa, he as much had a duty to address these matters. All this was campaign fodder for the opposition. The Patriotic Front rode on such inadequacies and made great gains by promising, if elected, to stop abusive investors and restricting foreign ownership of some sectors of the economy. That message sank deep into the working class and the result was seen in the manner urban dwellers balloted for the opposition party in the 2006 election. Call it a protest vote.

The baboon's face

Until four to five years after independence Zambia's economy was private sector-led. Under the Mulungushi Declaration of 1968 and the Matero Reforms of 1969, Kaunda nationalised the economy. The State took 51% shareholding in the mining industry, the backbone of the economy. Literature on this subject suggests there were two schools of thought. One is that Kaunda did it purely for political reasons, to endear himself to the masses following the turbulent political situation in UNIP between 1967 and 1968, owing to the rise of factions. Readers may wish to know that the bickering in UNIP then even led to Kaunda resigning, but he had to be persuaded to stay on. In the book *A Night without a President,* Sikota Wina gives the details. The other thinking is that it was only right to bring the economy in State hands and, by default, enable the people to share in the independence boom. Thus the long and short of it is that from 1969 to the early 1990s, it was government's business to be in business.

Top among the MMD economic reforms was liberalising the economy. In so doing, they enacted the Investment Act of 1992 to facilitate, coordinate and promote the establishment of business enterprises in Zambia; established the Lusaka Stock Exchange, enacted the Banking and Financial Acts of 1994 to strengthen the banking and financial sector; abolished foreign exchange controls, cut out subsidies and passed the Privatization Act No. 29 of 1992, which among other things, established the Zambia Privatization Agency (ZPA), a supposedly autonomous agency whose mandate was to implement the privatization programme. Specifically, its responsibilities were to plan, implement and control the privatization of State Owned Enterprises in cooperation with the government.

Zambia embarked on a privatisation programme dubbed the most ambitious in Africa. By the time Chiluba left office, save for what were 'strategic' industries, the majority of the economy was in private hands, a radical change from the commandist era when Zambia was one of the most nationalised economies on the continent.

Privatisation was an unpopular word, a synonym for joblessness and misery associated with the sale of state-owned firms. Andrew Chipwende, CEO of the ZPA, told an Economics Association of Zambia meeting on 11 February 2003 that about 105,000 jobs were lost through privatisation. However, it is important to look at privatisation objectively. It was not a complete failure as some of the privatised companies have to this day continued to perform exceptionally well. It is tempting to venture into the pros and cons of privatisation, but no, Satan, please go away.

By Mwanawasa's presidency, privatisation had been ongoing and hundreds of former parastatals had been turned over to the private sector. According to records from the now defunct ZPA, as at March 31, 2004, 259 formerly state-owned enterprises had been privatised out of a total portfolio of 282 companies. Apart from the mines, which were all sold by 2000, the sale of the three key parastatals, the Zambia National Commercial Bank, (Zanaco), the Zambia Electricity Supply Corporation (Zesco) and the Zambia Telecommunications Company (Zamtel), proved contentious. Zesco was "commercialised" under a World Bank plan in 2003, Zamtel remained. But the major privatisation issue that Mwanawasa had to deal with was Zanaco.

Meeting an IMF delegation at State House on 10 February 2003, he had serious misgivings about the manner in which privatisation had been conducted: "This issue as far as this administration is concerned is one which we support but we don't support the way it has been done because the result is that there has been no significant benefits to this country. Privatisation as has been done has contributed to high levels of poverty; it has contributed to asset stripping and a lot of other things."

Given the bad reputation privatisation had acquired, Mwanawasa opposed the sale of Zanaco. He said, "When I was elected President, one of the resolutions I made was to give privatisation a human face. I entertained great doubt about privatisation because many people lost employment. If Zanaco is to be sold, it should be sold with a human face. If it will be sold with a face of a baboon, I won't be part of it."

That position pleased the anti-privatisation advocates and for a while Mwanawasa won their support. This was the second attempt to halt the bank's sale. In March 2003 Parliament stopped the sale of Zanaco but the Executive later went ahead and advertised 51% shares with management rights. What some perhaps did not know was that the process of selling the bank had begun years earlier and Chiluba's government had already made a commitment to that effect via a Letter of Intent to the IMF. Undoing that would be an uphill battle. The IMF, which advocated for the sale of the bank, arm-twisted and pressured the government, reminding them of the earlier commitment.

In January 2007, as debate on the fate of the bank continued, Commerce Minister, Kenneth Konga told Parliament the dilemma government was in: "The credibility of Government would have been put on the line in view of the fact that we had an agreed programme with the International Monetary Fund. In turn, this would have affected the debt relief under the HIPC initiative. It should be pointed out that costs of losing credibility as a consequence of the reversal of the decision [to privatise the bank] would have likely been higher than the costs associated with the privatisation of the bank."

In his initial opposition, either Mwanawasa knew of the already existing agreement with the IMF and underestimated their doggedness thinking he could reverse that position, or he was oblivious to certain facts. He may have been sincere in his opposition, but the influence of the IMF was colossal and his government finally capitulated to their whims when the bank was sold for US$8 million to Rabobank of the Netherlands via the offer of 49% shares with a management takeover. Claims emerged that government had ignored advice on the sale of the bank and that there actually had been better local bidders. If true, this would be no surprise given the insistence of the IMF, whose chief interest was to have the bank in foreign hands. The unprecedented opposition to the bank's sale seen in mass demonstrations by civil society and other citizens showed just how much Zambians prized the bank. Needless to say it was sold against the will of the people.

In a sombre reflection, *The Post* newspaper, which was unrelenting in its opposition, stated:

> *It is sad that President Levy Mwanawasa and his government have totally ignored the will of the people over the issue of Zambia National Commercial Bank (ZNCB). While the people of Zambia made it very clear from the beginning that ZNCB should not be privatised, Levy and his government have instead opted to go with the demands of the International Monetary Fund (IMF) that this national bank should be sold. What is more sad, and perhaps an act of insincerity on the part of Levy, is his apparent numbness on this subject even when in August 2005 he agreed with many Zambians that there was no justification for the sale of ZNCB.*

Despite faltering in certain areas, Mwanawasa did try to rejuvenate the economy. Some of the plans were in their nascent stages and their fruits would only show in future. The efforts were worthwhile but the challenges were immense.

CHAPTER 12

THE SINKING TITANIC

"President Mugabe, arguing that only God can remove him from office, has publicly stated that he will not accept an MDC victory in the elections and has warned of a civil war led by the liberation veterans. This has created a state of fear among the Zimbabwe voters." –**Levy Mwanawasa, (1948-2008), 3rd President of Zambia, 2001-2008.**

STATE BANQUETS ARE normally characterised by diplomatic niceties where presidents talk economic and technical cooperation, mutual respect, co-existence and toast to warm relations and each other's good health. Yet it was at such an occasion in the Namibian capital, Windhoek where Mwanawasa made a major foreign policy pronouncement that effectively made him break ranks with other African leaders on a matter they had chosen to largely ignore.

The long story of how Robert Mugabe wrecked his country needs no repeat here. Cantankerous and unrepentant, he kept blaming his country's ills on the West, with former colonial power Britain being on the receiving end of his unrivalled vitriol. Amid a collapsed economy and chaotic politics, in which he brutalised his opponents and kept trampling on the people's fundamental freedoms, African leaders looked 'the other way'. African presidents are a brotherhood, they rarely criticise each other no matter how egregious the conduct.

So their complicity of silence on Mugabe was not entirely surprising, except its scale. But overlooking governance excesses in one country in the name of 'sovereignty' is an outdated tactic in modern international politics. In the 21st century, sovereignty is a fragile concept and the line between what is a domestic and what is a foreign issue has narrowed tremendously.

As United Nations Secretary-General, Kofi Annan had his own brush with Mugabe. In his memoirs *Interventions: A Life in War and Peace,* he writes:

> *Pressure from outside, among other African leaders, was slow in coming and feeble. This was largely because of the reverence in which Mugabe was held across Africa due to his heroic revolutionary achievements. Furthermore, he had directly helped the leaders of other freedom movements in the past, such as in Namibia, South Africa and Mozambique, whose governments were now run by the very same people. In the community of African leaders, he was effectively the foreman of a union of freedom fighters.*

It was against this background that, when Mwanawasa likened Zimbabwe to "a sinking titanic whose passengers are jumping out in a bid to save their lives", he became one of the very few African leaders to publicly criticise Mugabe. For once, an African leader was voicing out against another's impunity.

No respecter of reputations, Mwanawasa's position on Zimbabwe said much about how he was cut from a different ideological cloth. As other African leaders genuflected to the tyrant in tandem with the continent's deep-rooted "Big Man's" syndrome, Mwanawasa saw everything wrong, not only with Mugabe's misrule, but also with the manner his fellow leaders dealt with the matter.

When Mwanawasa took over the chair of the regional bloc Southern African Development Community (SADC) at the Lusaka summit in August 2007, then South African President Thabo Mbeki was the 'facilitator' of the 'Zimbabwe Dialogue', the protracted series of talks between the ruling ZANU-PF and the opposition Movement for Democratic Change (MDC). His approach had been widely criticised as permissive of Mugabe and unhelpful to the plight of Zimbabwe. But Mbeki's former aide Frank Chikane, in his memoirs *The Things That Could Not Be Said,* is glowing about Mbeki's role, describing it as something that "will go into the annals of history as one of the key elements of his legacy on the African continent."

Interestingly, Chikane notes that "after independence Zimbabwe had become the bright light of the southern African region and a reversal of its gains would impact negatively on the development of the rest of the region. In fact, it would be like turning off the light that gave hope to the rest of the continent."

What Chikane failed to acknowledge was that, as he accompanied Mbeki on his numerous trips to Harare, "the bright light of the southern African region" had long dimmed. Zimbabwe's economy lay on its deathbed. How that came to be is a subject Chikane conveniently evades.

The common narrative is that South Africa was grateful to Mugabe for delaying his land reform programme until after the end of apartheid. If he had done it before, it is believed, that would have sent the minority regime in Pretoria into panic, fearing it would suffer the same fate of land grabs once it handed over to the black majority. In effect, that would have delayed the end of apartheid. But however grateful South Africa was to Zimbabwe does not justify the manner Mbeki pandered to Mugabe, while overlooking the interests of the greater majority, millions of whom had fled the country.

Thus the difference in the approach to the Zimbabwe issue between Mbeki, the dialogue facilitator and Mwanawasa, the SADC chairperson couldn't have been evidently more different. While Mwanawasa may have been alive to that history, his political outlook and beliefs simply did not permit him to join the queue of African leaders cosying up to Mugabe for purely sentimental reasons.

Zimbabwe had continued to attract global attention and was the subject of discussion at various SADC summits. At the end of the 2007 Lusaka summit, the communiqué read:

> *The Summit was briefed that the negotiations between Zimbabwe African National Union-Patriotic Front (ZANU-PF) and both factions of the Movement for Democratic Change (MDC) were progressing smoothly. Summit commended President Thabo Mbeki. Summit welcomed the progress and encouraged the parties to expedite the process of negotiations and conclude work as soon as possible so that the next elections are held in an atmosphere of peace allowing the people of*

The Mwanawasa Years: An Analysis of his Presidency

Zimbabwe to elect the leaders of their choice in an atmosphere of peace and tranquillity.

Communiqués from presidential summits are notorious for recycling pious platitudes that do not reflect the intensity of discussions behind closed doors, nor the reality on the ground. SADC's wish that "the next elections are held in an atmosphere of peace" was too generous, especially knowing too well the sort of regime that held sway in Harare.

"Scandalous daylight robbery"

Before the Lusaka summit, MDC leader Morgan Tsvangirai and his team had been Mwanawasa's guests on more than one occasion. Tsvangirai came to Lusaka with two ideas. Firstly, he wanted to boycott the upcoming election; and secondly, he insisted on the 50% + 1 electoral threshold in the Constitution. "We advised him against both," revealed a former Cabinet minister who worked closely with Mwanawasa on the matter. "We told him that if he boycotted, he would become irrelevant. We also told him not to insist on that constitutional provision. We asked him, 'what if you win the first round? Don't you think you would have missed a chance to become President?'"

The general election took place on 29 March 2008. The election result took over a month to be announced, an enormous scandal for a small country like Zimbabwe. As electoral officials fiddled and shilly-shallied, word was already out that Mugabe had lost the election. In the meantime, Tsvangirai embarked on a tour of the region to drum up support for his supposedly incoming Presidency.

As fate would have it, the Lusaka prophecy came to pass. Tsvangirai won the first round of the election with 47.9%, against Mugabe's 43.2%, according to the Zimbabwe Electoral Commission. Tsvangirai however insisted he amassed 50.3%, claiming outright victory. "It's a scandalous daylight robbery," MDC spokesman Nelson Chamisa said. That claim aside, a second round was pending.

The Sinking Titanic

The ZANU-PF leadership met to digest the result. Rumours of a deal to facilitate Mugabe's exit swirled in the international media. In his book *The Fear: The Last Days of Robert Mugabe*, Peter Godwin recalls his excitement of a prospective post-Mugabe era:

> *I am on my way home to Zimbabwe, to dance on Robert Mugabe's political grave. Presidential elections, which he has fixed with ease in the past, using a combination of rigging, fraud and intimidation, have gone wrong. Zimbabweans have rejected him in such overwhelming numbers that he will finally be forced to accept their verdict. In a few days, he will meet his politburo to contemplate his own farewell. I've been anticipating this moment for so long.*

When Godwin gets the news from the ZANU-PF meeting that Mugabe has not conceded defeat, he realises that, after all "there is no political grave upon which to dance. What were we thinking? The old man isn't going anywhere, he'll die in office."

Then hell broke loose. Mugabe unleashed a reign of terror that forced Tsvangirai to abandon the second round. What had been the firmest rejection of Mugabe in nearly three decades eventually amounted to nothing. The autocrat had survived. Tsvangirai rued his chance.

Mwanawasa attempted to send a team of former heads of state to Zimbabwe, but the chaos and tension there made it impossible. He then summoned an Emergency Extraordinary Summit in May. Mugabe stayed away. On his way to Lusaka, Mbeki stopped over in Harare and, as if to embolden Mugabe, said "there's no crisis." It had been weeks and the election results had not been published even when it was already public knowledge that Mugabe had lost. There was tension in the country and violence was widespread. Kenyan Prime Minister Raila Odinga called for the suspension of Mugabe from the African Union until he held free and fair elections; Mandela decried "the tragic failure of leadership" in Zimbabwe, while ANC leader Jacob Zuma was even tougher in his assessment of the situation. Yet Mbeki saw no crisis.

To Harare's apprehension, Mwanawasa invited the MDC to the Emergency Extraordinary Summit.

"Mr Emmerson Mnangagwa who was leading the Zimbabwean delegation objected to the presence of the MDC. But President Mwanawasa took him on. He asked him how he thought SADC could help resolve the impasse without hearing from the other side," a former senior Cabinet minister who attended the meeting revealed. "Mwanawasa reminded him that when ZANU-PF was still a liberation movement before it became government, it was allowed to address the OAU. So he asked him, 'was that wrong'?"

He added: "President Khama [of Botswana] said since he had not heard from the MDC, he was interested in hearing from them. President Kikwete [of Tanzania] said the same. We were in the new building at the Mulungushi International Conference Centre. Then President Mwanawasa said those who wanted to listen to the MDC could move to the old building. Majority of the delegates moved there."

Then Foreign Affairs Minister Kabinga Pande gave a similar recollection of the proceedings. "It was a heated meeting that took us the whole night and I was only briefing the press at six in the morning," he said. "It got so acrimonious that I decided to send a note to President Mwanawasa to adjourn the meeting for tea just so that tempers could come down."

According to Pande, Zambia, Botswana and Tanzania took the same position and that incensed Mugabe. "They [Zimbabweans] treated us like we were hardliners. But President Mwanawasa said we could not pretend, he felt that as Chair of SADC he had to tell Zimbabwe the correct position."

Thus one thing the Extraordinary Summit achieved was Mwanawasa's prevailing over ZANU-PF in having the MDC present at the meeting.

Mwanawasa's courage knew no bounds. At a time when many African leaders kowtowed to Libya's Muammar Gaddafi, Mwanawasa chose not to. "There were few leaders who could tell off Gaddafi in his face and I know that as a result, Gaddafi didn't like President Mwanawasa," Pande revealed.

The Sinking Titanic

It is not every day that presidents publicly divulge happenings of their behind-the-scenes work. And when they do, something is amiss, unless it is nothing sensitive. At a June press conference, specifically to address the events playing out in Zimbabwe, Mwanawasa called for the postponement of the presidential run-off on the grounds that the conditions were not right for an election, referring to the SADC Principles and Guidelines Governing Democratic Elections. He recounted his repeated attempts to contact Mbeki but to no avail. His counterpart didn't return his phone calls, he said. His frustration was palpable and demonstrated once again their differences in the handling of the situation.

Mugabe and his ZANU-PF officials had for a long time adopted an exceptionally patronising position, in that whoever didn't agree with them on the handling of the situation in their country was 'a stooge of the West'. Consistent with that chant, they attacked Mwanawasa, accusing him of working with Western governments, whom Harare continually accused of imposing sanctions, even when the sanctions only applied to Mugabe and his cohorts. "I wish to urge authorities in Zimbabwe to exercise maximum restraint, especially during these trying times in their history, when dealing with SADC countries, including Zambia, for maintenance of peace and security," ZANU-PF official Patrick Chinamasa told the media.

But Mwanawasa refused to take the attack lying low. "Those are mere tantrums and they are not true," he shot back, adding that it would be "scandalous for SADC to keep quiet when things are not right in Zimbabwe."

As Mwanawasa prepared for the African Union summit in Egypt, the issue of Zimbabwe exercised his mind, former Cabinet minister Mike Mulongoti said.

> *I saw him two days before he left for the summit. He told me there were two people, one a Cabinet minister and another a former advisor to a former president who advised him not to talk about Zimbabwe at the summit. They believed that if he did, Mugabe would close the borders and strangle our economy. But he said he was not comfortable with that*

> advice. I was Minister of Information, so he asked me what he should say to journalists on arrival in Egypt. I told him, 'just say that your position on the matter is on record and that record has not changed.' He agreed and that was my last conversation with him.

Although he left the Zimbabwe issue unresolved, Mwanawasa had registered his position on the matter as being distinctly different from the rest of the African leaders. Various obituaries in the international press mentioned two issues on his legacy: his fight against corruption and his tough position on Zimbabwe.

Backed by an African Union summit resolution and using Kofi Annan's template that brought together Mwai Kibaki and Raila Odinga into a government of national unity after Kenya's 2007 disputed election, Mbeki went on to preside over the negotiation of an overstatedly named political settlement, the 'Global Political Agreement'. Like Odinga, Tsvangirai became the nominal Prime Minister. Given how close he came to being President, being Prime Minister with no real power simply amounted to seeking crumbs of relevance from Mugabe's table.

CHAPTER THIRTEEN

ONE MORE DUTY TO PERFORM

"The function of leadership is to produce more leaders, not more followers." - **Ralph Nader, American attorney and four-time candidate for President of the USA.**

GENERALLY, THE TREND across the world is that outgoing presidents like to leave the country with a leader of their choice. In my view, there are at least three main reasons for this tendency.

First, there are those who feel they have built an enviable track record that needs to be sustained and improved upon. They, therefore, feel duty bound to search for one whom they think will perfectly fit in with their scheme of operation and consolidate that record. They do not only want to be remembered for being good leaders, but also for having made sure they bequeathed to the country a leader who continued their good works.

Second, there are those who know that they dragged the country miles behind the starting line; they stole and mismanaged affairs of the State and thus annoyed the people who put them in office. They know that no one has any genuine regard for their governance profile. They reckon the only way to keep the lid on their misdeeds is to install one of like mind who is either a beneficiary of the loot, or who would be so eternally grateful for being handed the presidency that he will keep the dirt firmly under the carpet.

Third, there are those who remain so excessively inebriated with power that they can hardly imagine their time is up. While painfully coming to terms with the fact it's time to go, they would still want to have their hand in the affairs of the nation and acquire the status of a political godfather.

Agyeman-Duah gives another perspective to the problems of succession in Africa. He is so forthright that I yielded to the temptation of reproducing his observations here at length.

First is the absence of institutional framework for succession in many countries and, where the framework exists, its utter disregard by the leadership. Simply, the problem is symptomatic of authoritarian or totalitarian governance. In several such states and establishments leaders deliberately ignore this requirement and even make it a taboo to discuss succession plans.

Second are the cultural attitudes toward leadership in Africa. On one hand, political leaders tend to regard themselves as traditional rulers and want to be treated as such. Thus, they accept and often demand royal or chiefly treatment including accolades, appellations and the payment of homage. Under the pretext of promoting the national culture, leaders turn themselves literally into chiefs: to be greeted by a retinue, drumming and traditional incantations. This kind of treatment easily gets into their heads; they begin to see themselves as the "big chief" and, as you know, chiefs rule till death do them part!

On the other hand, the governed, that is, the people help the self-entrenchment of leaders by their attitude toward leadership. Besides the undue obsequiousness and platitudes, the governed typically sees the governor as the "Father of the Nation." The notion of a "father" has many imageries and expectations: a father is forever; you don't just push your father around; fathers like chiefs demand obedience and are not easily accountable. Combined with the chieftaincy images, the notion of a "father of the nation" leads to the promotion of personality cult. All such notions reinforce the permanent incumbency syndrome, an antithesis of democratic leadership.

The third explanation for the problem of leadership succession in Africa is the extensive powers that either the constitution or the lack of it gives to political leaders and the resultant patronage and patrimonial systems. Besides the extensive appointive powers of most African Executives, they also dominate law-making, control the national purse, and supervise the huge national development program, including the award of contracts. This overwhelming concentration of power enables the leader to create and preside over a system of patronage. The power to reward or sanction that turns subjects to supplicants reinforces the leader's feeling of indispensability and impregnability.

The general assumption is that the one anointed by the outgoing leader ordinarily stands a greater chance of getting the mantle. But that's only if the party membership decides to respect the incumbent's choice. If not, a split is inevitable as some members might find it offensive for one person to arbitrarily determine who should lead them, and by extension, the country. However much incumbents see it as their duty to choose a successor, this should not be their preserve but an openly agreed upon process in accordance with the laid-down rules supported by the majority.

For instance, history tells us that, looking back at her time in office as British Prime Minister, Margaret Thatcher said, "But there was one more duty I had to perform, and that was to ensure that John Major was my successor. I wanted to believe that he was the man to secure and safeguard my legacy and to take our policies forward." Major led the Conservatives until their defeat by "New Labour" in May 1997.

So it is not a sin for the outgoing leader to identify a successor and seek the support of members in getting that leader into power. What is politically sinful is pushing an agenda down the throat of others, in most cases for the personal benefit of the outgoing. There are leaders who know that the successors they are trying to prop up have no ability to govern a country. Yet they proceed to impose such leaders on the party and the country.

It is true that getting into power is a contest. Even those who get it on a silver plate have to fend off some opposition no matter how inconsequential. But what makes it sickening is that what should ideally be about ability and quality turns into a pedestrian affair. The clout the incumbent wields is such that he can choose to burden the country with the most inept leader if that will serve his interests. Those who have been close to the master assume it is their right to receive the long-awaited prize for loyalty, while those who have been distant do their utmost to endear themselves to the master in desperate anticipation that they get the anointment. Thus when the incumbent's time nears the end, a protracted fight for the anointing hand ensues. There is massive lobbying, jockeying and jostling and the incumbent's anointing hand is so powerful that it can sometimes decide the fate of a nation.

The history of succession in Zambia is a mixed one. By virtue of the political system in place between 1972 and 1990, Kaunda kept succeeding himself both as party and national President. He 'contested' alone and voters were only asked to say 'yes' or 'no'. That Kaunda would win was never in doubt, only by what margin. Using both manipulation and high-handedness, Chiluba had an easy ride throughout his ten years, facing practically no opposition to his hold on the party and national presidency. But because he was determined to latch on longer than was legally required and politically desirable, he had no succession plan for the party, and by extension, the country. His choice of Mwanawasa was but a 'crash project' after the people overthrew his ambition of a third term.

Internal battles

Since Mwanawasa made it clear he would not add his name to the 'list of shame' of some African leaders who had turned the Presidency into an institution of personal dominion, Zambians could look forward to how the succession battle would pan out. Moments before he fell ill in Sharm-el-Sheikh, he ventured into the subject.

Kabinga Pande was the last Cabinet minister with Mwanawasa. "We were chatting in the hotel lobby while waiting to have meetings with other heads of state. That day he talked a lot about governance and leadership. He said 2011 appeared too far away and he wondered how some African leaders had managed to stay in power for a long time."

In earlier public statements, he told the corrupt never to contemplate offering themselves as his successors. Agreed, this was in line with his anti-corruption zeal but it was also hypocritical because he had worked with some of the corrupt elements in the party while they appeared in court on corruption charges. Some of them had even helped him campaign and played a part in his being President. Was their holding of party positions while charged with corruption a lesser evil?

The race was wide open. But since Mwanawasa did not preside over the selection or election of his successor, we can only imagine how differently the battle might have panned out if he were around. His death created a free-for-all affair and there was little regard for what plans he may have had.

Mwanawasa suffered a stroke while attending an African Union summit in Egypt in June 2008. He lay in a Paris hospital until he died on 19 August. With no party vice president and with the rest of the leadership at the mercy of scheming factions, the party was essentially leaderless. Then national chairman Michael Mabenga tried to hold the fort but it was being tossed and turned by the jostling brigade.

Zambian political parties have a long way to go in preparing for succession. At any given time you will not find a political party with a known succession plan. That explains the confusion that arises when a leader vacates office unexpectedly.

Mwanawasa attempted to deal with succession early enough. He still had three years of his second term. Interviews with some of his former ministers revealed that he had already identified potential successors. Therefore, it can be said that the confusion that arose after his death could not necessarily be blamed on the lack of an already confirmed successor because, as revealed by insiders, a process of identifying a successor was in place three years ahead of Mwanawasa's exit. Nature just struck too soon.

On a sunny Tuesday morning under the shade of palm trees at her farmhouse in Lusaka, Mutale Nalumango told me she was "professionally close enough" to Mwanawasa to have known first-hand his views on some issues. She narrated: "I met him at his home two months before he died. He referred to a stroke he suffered in 2006. He said 'the next time it recurs it will

175

be fatal.' I moved him away from that topic. Then we turned to the issue of succession. He told me he had three people in mind, Magande, Pande and Chilala. I gave him my views on each one of them. But whether between the time I talked to him and the time he died he came up with other plans, I am not sure, but I doubt."

At the time, Kabinga Pande was Foreign Minister, Kasempa MP and MMD deputy national chairperson; Magande was Finance Minister, Chilanga MP and MMD chairperson for economy and finance. Costain Chilala is a commercial farmer based in Mkushi.

Almost everyone I interviewed on succession mentioned the same three names as having been considered by Mwanawasa. Seated in the busy and noisy lobby at Parliament on a rainy Wednesday afternoon, Pande told me a lot about his experiences with Mwanawasa but when it came to confirming if the President had let him in on succession, he was self-effacing and cagy.

"I can neither confirm nor deny," he told me, suppressing a smile which simply gave him away.

"There were so many things he told me, some of which I cannot disclose because they were in confidence," he said in an evasive response to my question. "But one thing I can reveal he told me was that he would not want to leave a crook or a tribalist in State House."

The former Foreign Minister strongly downplayed suggestions that he was among the ministers closest to Mwanawasa. "I can never make that claim because I don't know who else the President met and what they discussed."

Repeated attempts to meet Chilala failed. But according to some of his close associates, it is highly unlikely he would have agreed to stand as president. "He strictly shuns the limelight and has no interest in politics," one of them said. "He is more at home inspecting crops and talking with his workers than addressing crowds and making appeals."

"As you may recall, the last time he was in the public domain was when he was board chairperson of the Food Reserve Agency. After that, you don't hear of him often," another said.

Besides being a stranger to politics, Chilala would have been a total stranger to the MMD. Even those who confirmed Mwanawasa had him on his list could not quite comprehend why.

According to Nalumango, some senior members of the party and government went to test their luck with Mwanawasa. "There are some colleagues I know who were interested in succeeding him. They went and asked him, 'what about me Mr. President?' His response was, 'It's a democracy, you are free to stand but I won't support you'. That was Mwanawasa for you,"she said, before bursting into laughter.

A presidential election was due within ninety days of Mwanawas's death according to the Constitution. As the succession battle ensued, Magande's name flashed. From the interviews I conducted, there were those who vouched for Magande as Mwanawasa's last choice and those who disapproved of the claim, insisting that while Magande was among the potentials, it would be preposterous for anyone to claim he was the anointed one.

"President Mwanawasa told me Mr Magande was among the people he was considering," Gabriel Namulambe said. "But when he died we looked at the situation and we decided that Mr Rupiah Banda who was Vice President should finish the remaining three years."

Whether Magande was abandoned or a victim of the changed circumstances is open to debate. But it can also be said that those who may have felt compelled to support him because he was a 'Mwanawasa candidate' may have now felt more liberated to switch loyalty and back Banda.

Mulongoti says he had a difficult time convincing Banda to contest. "He was saying he was too old and that many people thought he was UNIP and therefore felt he couldn't make it," he said. "He was also scared of losing to Mr Sata. That he told me."

Mulongoti also revealed his differences with Magande. "When we were in a Cabinet meeting, he accused me of standing in his way [to be president]. Since I was Minister of Information, he also accused me of blocking the media from covering him. Mr Banda [who was acting President at the time] was chairing the meeting and he asked me to respond. I said, 'we have a very short time to prepare for this election. We have three years before the end of our mandate. We should use the benefit of incumbency. All of you who want to stand should wait for 2011'. That didn't go down well with him," he narrated. "That is how I supported Banda. Both Magande and Banda were outsiders but the difference was that Banda was Vice President and we could use his position to our advantage. We did that and won the election."

Nalumango gave another perspective: "Banda was not among the people Mwanawasa was considering. But I voted for him when we met as National Executive Committee. Magande is a great Zambian, he loves Zambia, he is passionate about development, he is well educated and has a lot of experience. If there are Zambians who should be helping run this country, Magande is one of them. But I doubted his ability to carry the crowd."

Kalala remembers Mwanawasa saying in a Cabinet meeting that he didn't appoint Banda as Vice President to take over from him. "That sounded awkward but that was how frank he was. In the evening, he phoned Mr Banda to explain that he didn't mean to offend him. His reasoning was that Kaunda was succeeded by someone younger and the same for Chiluba. So he simply wanted to continue that trend."

However, Magande was a year older than Mwanawasa and would not represent a generational change of leadership. So the issue of him being a younger successor was not correct, except in comparison to Banda. Banda himself had said on several occasions that he had no intentions of being President. He made the political comeback only because Mwanawasa invited him to.

Kalala said National Executive Committee members knew Mwanawasa's view. "The Magande issue was not a rumour. I discussed it with Mwanawasa at Nkwazi House and I told him if he wanted someone who would continue with his vision and programmes, it was Magande," he stressed. "When we were in Botswana, Mwanawasa told Magande that he was known in international circles but that he needed him to be known inside the country. As part of the plan to prepare Magande, Mwanawasa was about to move him from Finance to Agriculture. Many people would have interpreted that as a demotion. But the idea was to give Magande a chance to meet the ordinary people and we thought the Ministry of Agriculture would give him that chance."

Magande may have had the upper hand as long as Mwanawasa was around, but unfortunately, post-Mwanawasa, he did not have the support of his colleagues. That meant he lost before the vote. Whether he would have suffered the same fate if Mwanawasa were around is now a matter of conjecture.

I contacted Magande but he informed me that he was writing his memoirs which would include his experiences with Mwanawasa. Therefore, he said, he would reserve his story for his readers, a position I understood much as I would have loved him to say something here.

But Mwanawasa's choice of Magande presented an interesting perspective. It appears in settling for a successor, Mwanawasa was influenced by his own world view of politics. He was seemingly attracted to Magande for his economic management skills. Winning an election, however, requires more than that. Neither man was a grassroots politician who could rally the masses, they both lacked the common touch with the mechanics of everyday politics.

Mwanawasa was a high flying lawyer who came to government preaching morality and good governance, not a bad thing in itself. But he possessed no gift of the gab and therefore had difficulties connecting with the people. Magande was a bureaucrat habituated to the realm of economic policy and gracing corridors of the international financial community. When he came into Mwanawasa's circle, he was locked up in the Treasury with his fellow number crunchers, away from the political floor where the fight for power plays out. That may explain Kalala's proposition that Mwanawasa thought Magande needed to be marketed in-country.

Generally, finance ministers are seen as detached from the realities on the ground and are mostly accused of pursuing economic policies that hurt the poor. They are looked at as some kind of 'hatchet men', people whom Presidents send to announce the unpopular concerning the economy. With this in mind, how did Mwanawasa hope to sell Magande?

Further, Magande was a newcomer to the MMD, the same tag Mwanawasa had when he returned in 2001. Did he want to continue the trend where 'newcomers' took over? Would the old guards have accepted or simply acquiesced out of fear of Mwanawasa? What effect would that have had on the internal politics of the party? Would Mwanawasa have been the real power behind a Magande Presidency by running the show remotely?

As noted earlier, it's not a political sin for the outgoing leader to identify a successor, as Thatcher did with Major, for instance. But it is important to build consensus in finally arriving at that choice. Inasmuch as Magande was said to have been Mwanawasa's choice, the rate at which his colleagues 'abandoned' him after Mwanawasa's death was perhaps an indication of the task Mwanawasa would have had convincing them about his choice. But all this is in retrospect.

CHAPTER FOURTEEN

REFLECTIONS

"Effective leadership is not about making speeches or being liked; leadership is defined by results, not attributes." - **Peter Ferdinand Drucker (1919 – 2005), management consultant and author.**

WHAT DID MWANAWASA set out to achieve in his Presidency? How do the people he worked with judge him? Where did he succeed? Where did he fail? What could he have done differently or better?

"Mwanawasa and I agreed that we would campaign on three things. First, to give Zambia a new Constitution, second, to have zero tolerance against corruption and, third, to unite the country," recollected Mbita Chitala. "I mentioned those three things in front of his wife as she made me tea, you can ask her," he added, as if to emphasise the gravity.

I contacted Mrs Maureen Mwanawasa to seek her insight on a number of issues including how she felt when her husband overruled people floating her as a successor. But the process of getting an appointment proved long even as my deadline loomed.

According to Chitala, Mwanawasa planned to serve for only five years, in which he would achieve the three targets. "But how he changed to run for a second term, I don't know," he strongly disclaimed, shaking his head gently as he leaned back in his chair.

What is your verdict of his Presidency, I asked him. "Mwanawasa did very well in the first five years. But as his health began to fail him, people took advantage of him and he started making mistakes," reflected the former presidential campaign manager. "Certain bad habits started coming up. Tribalism appeared to be on the ascendancy. He failed to deliver the Constitution. I could see corruption emerging and I could see nepotism coming on the scene again when we had agreed on meritocracy."

On the flipside, Chitala thinks Mwanawasa was "a nice, honest person who wanted to give his best to Zambia." He blames the failures of Zambian presidents on too much power derived from a bad Constitution. "You can't have a President with so much power. That is why we need a Constitution that distributes power. We need to hide in the Constitution to safeguard us against individuals."

Chitala is right about the need for strong systems and institutions and the need to redistribute power. But considering how well-versed Mwanawasa was with the law, as well as the eloquence with which he discussed the need for a good Constitution, it would have been interesting to know whether he believed it hindered his progress or made him fail in certain respects. What is true, however, is that his failures had more to do with his inability to push through his agenda than legal barriers that stood in his way or legal loopholes he may have exploited.

Kavindele said Mwanawasa succeeded in trying to instil discipline in the work culture in government. "There are so many things we see now which under Mwanawasa would cause heads to roll," he said. "He was committed to his job and he was genuinely concerned about the welfare of the people. Things such as high prices and the cost of living concerned him."

This book is not about Mwanawasa the individual, the husband, the father, brother, uncle or nephew. It is about Mwanawasa the President, his government, its policies, decisions, successes and failures. I wrote on his Presidency as an attempt to document the key features that characterised his tenure and the lessons they provided. The little the book says about his personality is merely meant to give a brief background of the person who later became Zambia's third President. Leaders make decisions that affect the life of the people and the destiny of a country. This book sought to bring into perspective some of the decisions Mwanawasa made, what purpose they served and what effect they had on Zambia.

So much good has been said about Mwanawasa, especially after his death. It is understood that we live in a society where it is considered improper and culturally ill-mannered to criticise the dead. But in my analysis, I have chosen to depart from that long-established tradition. Pierre-Augustin Caron de Beaumarchais (1732–1799), a French publisher, once said, "Without the freedom to criticise, there can be no true praise."

Mwanawasa was an unpopular leader. Firstly, his ascendancy to the MMD presidential candidacy in 2001 caused quite a lot of confusion in the party. Having resigned from government in 1994, he was something of an outsider when he returned. Secondly, his ascendancy to the State presidency was equally controversial because of the disputed election. Thirdly, once he was in the driving seat, his decisions were incessantly criticised.

In death, however, Mwanawasa enjoys a very high approval rating, admired for his courage and decisiveness, having redefined the Presidency in his own way. There were glowing tributes at his passing. "A gallant lawyer", "a great man who stood for the ideals of the legal profession", "a frank and honest leader", "a defender of democracy", "a paradigm of excellence."

It is interesting that a leader who took off on a very challenging note, who had difficulties connecting with the people, who was ceaselessly criticised ended up being the most praised and remembered. Perhaps there's something Zambian (or human) about posthumous eulogies. "He once told me Zambians would only appreciate his efforts when he was gone," recalled Pande.

Most of the people I interviewed, including those who were critical of his decisions, say Mwanawasa gave his best and always sought to do an honest job but was let down by those he entrusted with certain responsibilities. Nowhere was this view more overwhelming than on the fight against corruption. Therefore, they say, his failures were not necessarily of his own making. That is a fair proposition. The Presidency is a vast political and administrative machinery in which the incumbent cannot check on every cog and gear; sometimes he can only assume that those under his charge are promoting his mission. But this assumption is not always correct, not even in the world's most powerful government.

For instance, former US Secretary of State Colin Powell says President Richard Nixon would issue directives and no one knew what, if anything, happened to his orders. As a White House Fellow in 1973, Powell was given the job of finding out. "The people elect a President to run the country, but Presidents soon discover that they don't necessarily control the machinery of government," Powell notes in his autobiography *My American Journey*.

That, truly, is the dilemma presidents face. But in the end, it is an individual's record that is judged and the buck, unfortunately, stops with the individual who happens to be President. When people pass judgment on a President, regrettably, they do so without being privy to what they cannot see. Thus, no matter how harsh the public's judgment, sometimes the President has to take it as it comes. The President does not have the time to explain or justify every decision.

Harry Truman said, "If the President knows what he wants, no bureaucrat can stop him. A President has to know when to stop taking advice." In *My Life*, Bill Clinton says, "One of the most important decisions a President has to make is when to take the advice of the people who work for him and when to reject it. Nobody can be right all the time, but it's a lot easier to live with bad decisions that you believe in when you made them than with those your advisors say are right but your gut says are wrong."

Through the narrative and interactions with Mwanawasa's associates and subordinates, a premise has been established of what he stood for and what he wanted to achieve. But since this is a posthumous account, we cannot know or tell for sure when, or if, Mwanawasa rejected or stopped taking advice, or whether bureaucrats stood in his way and thereby undermined his ability to achieve his goals. Only he could say so with certainty.

Leadership and decision-making are synonymous. At whatever level of leadership, leaders are required to make decisions. A docile and indecisive leader is the last thing most people are prepared to tolerate. Some of the decisions leaders make during their tenure will be popular and will endear them to their followers. However, it is the not-so-popular ones that make the task of leadership challenging. It is also worth noting that not all unpopular decisions are necessarily bad. It may take years, mostly when the leader is long gone, for people to appreciate that the unpopular decision made at the time was for the public good.

Mwanawasa may have acted in what he thought was in the best interest of the nation, but his decisions may not always have been appreciated. He made popular and unpopular decisions that earned him admirers and critics alike. Just as the surgeon cannot guarantee 100% success in an operation, so it is with leadership and decision-making. Failures are bound to occur.

In some of the decisions he took, Mwanawasa exhibited rare courage. The boldness with which he pursued the corrupt, even at the expense of political support, is an obvious example. As a result, by the time he vacated office, he had succeeded in placing the fight against corruption as a core governance theme in addition to other governance reforms that he undertook. He demonstrated that it is possible to build a society in which corruption and the corrupt are detested rather than tolerated and glorified; where laws prevail over individuals' say-so.

Despite the high poverty levels which he painfully acknowledged, Mwanawasa presided over a period of relative economic stability and prosperity, backed by policy consistency and economic planning. His decision to take on the powerful mining circuit over taxes once again demonstrated his mettle to run against the grain and confront issues head-on.

However, his failure to deliver the Constitution is a blight on his record, especially given the thoughtfulness he displayed on the matter. Had he delivered it, his legacy would have been a notch up. Further, the rise of tribalism and nepotism under a leader who had expressed so much abhorrence for corruption was a contradiction which his critics gladly used to whip him.

Unlike in earlier centuries when monarchies held sway, the system of governance across much of the world now is that the majority choose, through elections, a few individuals to preside over national affairs, guided by a framework of laws and institutions. It is, therefore, incumbent upon those entrusted with such an honour to act in the interest of the people. They should bear in mind that they exist only as proxies and merely on the basis of trust, which can be revoked when the people so desire.

APPENDIX 1:

MWANAWASA'S INAUGURAL SPEECH ON 2 JANUARY 2002

I feel extremely honoured and humbled by the enormous responsibility bestowed upon me today to lead Zambia as president of the republic in the next 5 years.

It is befitting that I take oath of office here on the steps of the Supreme Court of Zambia, as we have always done, to reflect the dignity with which we hold our judiciary as a mirror of the national spirit.

I extend special thanks to Dr Chiluba who has steered this country for the past 10 years in peace and tranquillity. We have had a peaceful and successful election... Let me at this juncture as well, extend an invitation to Dr K. D. Kaunda, the founding father of our nation, to make himself available when need arises to advise me and the new administration...

I wish to pledge to do my best to ensure that the mandate entrusted to our country - namely, to facilitate and manage the transformation process from the O.A.U. into the African Union is fulfilled.

To our colleagues in the region I wish to assure you that my administration will continue to pursue the policy of peace, friendship and good neighbourliness. We shall respect the independence, sovereignty and territorial integrity of all our neighbours.

In this regard, we shall not allow our territory to be used by, nor shall we support, any group seeking to overthrow a government through unconstitutional means in any of our neighbouring countries.

In turn, we expect all our neighbours to treat and relate to us in similar manner...

I promise you countrymen and women of Zambia, that... We intend to implement the programmes in our manifesto, and emphasize the new change which will be a more human centred process. By this we mean, we will focus on the Zambian people as both the end and the means of development...

In The New Deal, agriculture shall be at the centre stage of our economic development policy. Agricultural programmes will aim at ensuring food security in both rural and urban areas; and in creating employment. We have to give a new look at agriculture since copper cannot be relied upon to be a continuing engine of development and employment.

We aim to boost or encourage investment both foreign and local, individually or foreign capital in partnership with local capital.

We will strive to enable as many of our people as possible, wherever they are, to access goods and services to satisfy their basic needs... there should be enough food for families, better housing and essential services, such as clean water, sanitation, public transport, education and health services...

As we seek to increase national productivity, my administration is conscious of the need to harness the talents and potential of all our people. We shall, therefore, ensure that our job creation efforts take into account the need to include the women, the disabled and the youth...

I am aware, fellow citizens, of the suffering that retirees go through as a result of delays in paying them their pension benefits...

The current tax regime has placed a heavy burden on the people and the business sector. It is, therefore, the intention of my government to... establish a tax regime that facilitates rather than hinders local productivity...

These elections have come and gone. Many lessons have been learnt. It is my sincere hope that as Zambians we shall all bury our differences and march forward together...

To my colleagues who aspired for this position, I salute you and respect you for the good fight we had. Now the nation needs your positive contribution because we all want a better life for our people...

I promise to be president for all the people, whether you voted for me or not, whether you voted for MMD or not, whether you did not vote or did not even register as a voter I am president for all of you, the people of Zambia.

I will provide continuity with change... I pray for your support and cooperation in this task... Long live Zambian democracy.

APPENDIX TWO
(MWANAWSA'S LAST SPEECH IN ZAMBIA)

SPEECH BY HIS EXCELLENCY DR. LEVY P. MWANAWASA, SC, PRESIDENT OF THE REPUBLIC OF ZAMBIA AT THE OFFICIAL OPENING OF THE ASSOCIATION OF MEMBER EPISCOPAL CONFERENCES IN EASTERN AFRICA (AMECEA) PLENARY ASSEMBLY MULUNGUSHI INTERNATIONAL CONFERENCE CENTRE, LUSAKA, ZAMBIA 28ᵀᴴ JUNE, 2008

I greet you all in the name of the Prince of Peace and the citadel of justice, our saviour the Lord Jesus Christ. I am greatly humbled to welcome all of you, particularly our visitors to Zambia, the land we proudly call *"The Real Africa"*, the seat of African liberation and peace. Zambia is so-named because of our internationally unrivalled hospitality and tradition of peaceful co-existence amid cultural and political diversity. Yes, we are proud of one of our greatest assets, the friendliness and warmth of our people, even in the face of the current cold weather. I am sure you will all take time to prove me right during the course of your deliberations here in Lusaka, if you have not yet done so.

On behalf of the government, the people of Zambia, and indeed on my own behalf, I say to you, dear brothers and sisters in Christ, *"Karibuni Sana"*. Against this background, your eminences, distinguished AMECEA bishops, it is only right and fitting that you should converge in Zambia under the theme *"reconciliation through justice and peace"*. Indeed, I am briefed that Zambia was chosen to host this particular assembly on this theme for two main reasons.

Firstly, it is because the Zambian Catholic Church has a very vibrant justice and peace ministry. As president of Zambia today, I can confidently confirm that because I have on several occasions felt the vibrancy of this ministry. Whether or not it has always made me comfortable is another matter!!!

Secondly, it is because Zambia has been recognised as a peaceful country that has withstood the challenges of diversity, holding itself together since independence without any civil strife. This is, of course, commendable in comparison to what we have seen in many other parts of the world. For this great gift of peace, we are eternally thankful to God our Father. It is always our prayer that our nation will always remain united even in the face of serious challenges of poverty as a result of uneven development, especially between our rural and urban areas. Your decision to hold this important assembly in our country will keep us encouraged to stay the course of peace and to do everything in our power, with God's help, to export this rare humane commodity to the rest of Africa and the entire world. I beg all of you to keep us in your prayers as we aspire to be the *"light and salt"* of the earth as our Lord Jesus Christ commanded us to be.

My dear brothers and sisters in Christ, Zambia's peaceful disposition did not come by accident. For many years, it has been anchored on our historical readiness for dialogue and reconciliation whenever we have been faced with a situation of potential conflict. Those who have taken the trouble to read Zambia's political history will recall that the first Zambian coalition government of 1962 was born out of reconciliation between Dr. Kenneth Kaunda and Mr. Harry Mwaanga Nkumbula. As you will recall, the two leaders had earlier been serious political rivals. By forming the coalition between their political parties in the interest of the nation, they effectively defeated the European-dominated **United Federal Party (UFP)**, defining the path to our political independence in 1964. In the same nationalist spirit, **The Choma Declaration** of 27th June, 1973 was proclaimed by the same two heroic leaders of our history to curb the then rising political strife in our country.

Let me remind our fellow citizens that we are greatly blessed to have this plenary in Zambia today when we are celebrating twenty five years or the silver jubilee of the Choma Declaration which fell only yesterday. More recently, in 1990, we once again saw the Zambian reconciliatory spirit when Dr. Kenneth Kaunda, in the face of the rising demand for multi-partyism, called for multi-

Appendix 2

party elections in 1991, thus curtailing his own presidential term by two years. He went further to peacefully hand over power to Dr. Frederick Chiluba and the MMD following his electoral defeat in those epoch-making elections that opened doors to the democratisation process on the African continent.

Allow me to say today, what a blessed nation we are for having had a selfless leadership from the beginning of our nationhood. Thus, the only way that I could appreciate the great contribution of Dr. Kenneth Kaunda to the peace of our country was to confer upon this great son of Africa the honour to be **Grand Officer of the Eagle of Zambia, First Division**, the highest honour that a Zambian head of state can confer. This was in no way meant to recompense him for all his heroic works in the history of our nation. No. far from it. There could be no price good enough to cover the personal sacrifices that went with the struggle for our freedom and the freedom of our neighbouring countries in this region. It was simply to say *"thank you, father of our nation, for what you have done for us and for our continent."*

Fellow Christians, what then is reconciliation? The Collier's dictionary defines the word "reconcile" as *"to make friendly again or win over a friendly attitude; to settle a quarrel or dispute; to make arguments, ideas, texts, accounts, etc, consistent, compatible, etc; to bring into harmony".* In the *"catechism of the Catholic Church"* by Pauline's Publications Africa, 1994, we are taught that reconciliation denotes forgiveness, man's acceptance of his sinful nature and God's readiness to forgive.

Through the *sacrament of penance,* the sinner confesses his or her sins by disclosing them to God, thus acknowledging and praising the holiness of God and his mercy towards sinful man. Through the priest's sacramental solution, God grants pardon and peace to the penitent or the one who confesses their sins. From this teaching therefore, it is clear that reconciliation cannot happen in the absence of confession which can only occur upon recognition of and regret for one's wrong-doing. And in the absence of reconciliation, there can be no peace and no forgiveness from God!! In The Holy Bible, in Matthew chapter 5 verses 22 to 24, it is written:

> *"I say to you, whoever is angry with his bother [or indeed, sister] will be liable to judgment... therefore, if you bring your gift to the altar, and there you recall that your brother has anything against you, leave your gift there at the altar, go first and be reconciled with your bother, and then come and offer your gift."*

My dear brothers and sisters, this teaching tells us that without reconciliation amongst ourselves, our prayers to God will not be answered. We must therefore do first things first: reconcile then seek the face of God when the Lord Jesus Christ taught us how to pray, he instructed us to say*: "forgive us our trespasses as we forgive those who trespass against us"* (Luke chapter 11 verse 4 and Matthew chapter 6 verse 12). This is reconciliation, a give-and-take process. It is founded on love which, according to Romans chapter 13 verse 10*, "does no evil to the neighbour."*

My dear brothers and sisters, from Zambia's political background that I have just recounted, it should not surprise any of us when we look at the recent political developments in our country. I am referring here to the now infamous reconciliation between myself and the Patriotic Front leader, Mr. Michael Sata. This is not a strange phenomenon. It is the normal way that we Zambians have historically dealt with conflict. For the purpose of our visitors, Bembas and Ngonis fought bitter tribal wars. I don't want to judge as to who the winner was, but I will leave that to Archbishop Mpundu and Bishop Lungu to resolve. One thing I will guarantee you, however, is that the two church leaders will not agree as to what the result of the war was, but ironically, they will embrace each other after a long argument. When a relative of one of them dies, the other one, with all his relatives, will take over the funeral proceedings that will effectively lighten the burden of the other.

What I am saying, dear brothers and sisters, is that out of that bitter tribal war was born one of the best inter-tribal relationships in our country. From my bitter quarrels with Mr. Sata, a time had to come when it had to stop in the interest of peace in our country. As it were, the reconciliation process had to be stimulated by a life-threatening situation. Whether good or bad is not for me to judge but I believe God has a plan for everything.

Many of you will recall that in my inaugural speech for my second presidential term at Parliament buildings on 3rd October 2006, I emphatically stated:

"... This is my final presidential term. I have a dream to leave Zambia even greater than before you elected me in 2001. However, I will only do so with your support and commitment. I would like to leave a legacy of the rule of law. I would like to leave a culture where national debate is not about assassinating each other's characters but a search for solutions to the problems that affect the weakest members of our society ... [however] our efforts will not yield much if they are not founded on strong feelings of love for one another and a strong commitment to national unity ...let us all unite to create a better Zambia ... we need each other to succeed".

Hence, my dear brothers and sisters, if you had read the letter and spirit of my speech on that great day, this development should not surprise or unsettle you. Fellow Christians, I do not say this to seek praise and reward. Nay. The people of Zambia have rewarded me enough by making me their top servant, an honour for which I will always remain truly grateful. Neither do I wish to claim total innocence in some of the political differences that we may have experienced during my presidency. Human as I am, I have probably contributed as much to these differences as my colleagues in the opposition but this has not in any way subtracted from my innermost desire for political tolerance and tranquility. To Catholic priests and senior clergy, this may sound like a confession though it may fall short of the strict criteria of a Catholic penitential rite. Allow me, nevertheless, to say my absolution in the words of one old philosopher, John Milton, who said, *"what in me is dark, illuminate; what in me is low, raise and support."*

Let me take this opportunity to thank my brother, Michael Sata for having demonstrated humility and magnanimity as we lead the people of Zambia to greater prosperity within our plural political dispensation. This means that all political parties in Zambia, including the MMD and the Patriotic Front, will, at least in the foreseeable future, remain independent of each other and compete for the people's vote in all elections. Our independence will guarantee accountability in public office through checks and balances, the critical role that is traditionally played by opposition parties in multi-party political systems like ours.

Of the citizens of this country, therefore, I only ask your patience to allow this process to work. From the church, both Catholic and other denominations, I ask not for your condemnation but for your understanding and prayers for the healing that this nation so desperately needs to maintain our peaceful ways. The challenges that the theme of this plenary pose to Africa and the world at large are enormous, to say the least. Today, we live in a world torn apart by conflict; a world dominated by hatred, war and civil strife. This challenges the Christian world to be the ***light and salt*** of the earth. Today, we have a great opportunity to translate the teachings of our Lord Jesus Christ, the Prince of Peace, into practical realities.

We can either grasp this opportunity or squander it and face judgment when that day comes. To promote love, we must embrace reconciliation which, unfortunately, is a hard and painful process but with no escape routes or shortcuts. It calls us to engage our adversaries in constructive dialogue whose only outcome is peaceful co-existence and socio-economic progress. The earlier that we African political leaders recognise the need for reconciliation, the better for our peoples. Unnecessary conflict will only retard our continent and drive our nations into further poverty and squalor.

Fellow Christians, is it not a serious contradiction and utter hypocrisy that although Christianity is growing in Africa, we Africans continue to hate each other with passion? How can one explain the recent xenophobic, now being referred to afri-phobic, attacks in the Republic of South Africa? I do not want to believe that this is the South African way of expressing gratitude to other African nations that sacrificed so much in the anti-apartheid struggle. God forbid! There is clearly something amiss which calls for urgent and serious resolution. Your Graces, Your Lordships, fellow Christians, Africa today faces an uphill battle in ensuring justice in our governance systems, and Zambia is no exception. We cannot claim to entrench justice in our governance processes in the face of high poverty levels especially in our rural areas. According to the living conditions survey of 2006, poverty levels in Zambia stand at 64 percent. In rural areas, poverty stands at a staggering 80 percent. Although we have worked hard to reduce the levels from 73 percent in 1998 to the current levels, I have always admitted that this situation is clearly unsatisfactory.

In my address at the official opening of the **National Indaba** on 17th October, 2003, I regretted the high incidence of poverty in our country despite our rich natural resource endowment. I observed that the fight against poverty was not a preserve of government alone. I therefore called on all our people - political parties, civil society, the church, the labour movement, the business community and the entire citizenry to unite in ensuring that we defeat poverty and bring back dignity to all our people. I am pleased to note that we are now working in tandem but a lot still remains to be done if we are to guarantee sustained peace and justice in our land. I believe that the church and state share a common, unique and historical calling – that of striving to constantly lift our people from hunger, illiteracy and disease.

Today, we are confronted by the HIV/AIDS pandemic which threatens our very own existence as humanity, hence raising the stakes for greater co-operation between us. Despite the fact that we may sometimes disagree as church and state, we are inextricably intertwined and we owe it to our people to strengthen our partnership in the fight against poverty. Although the challenge of poverty still remains in our midst, I am consoled to note that the situation in Africa and in particular, the AMECEA region, is slowly improving. It will obviously take some time for the current positive economic indicators to translate into the desired results for our people to directly experience at both personal and household levels. I am optimistic, however, that, with God's help and patience on the part of our people, we shall certainly get there.

Allow me to acknowledge, at this point, the tremendous work that the Catholic Church has done and continues to do in the socio-economic areas of our country. Here, I have in mind your great contribution in the education and health sectors since the dawn of Christianity in our country. I also gratefully acknowledge your outstanding advocacy for debt cancellation through the Jubilee 2000 campaign.

Today, our country is recording positive economic growth rates, partly as a result of the debt cancellation that we received with your full support. I urge you to use your power this time around to wage another campaign for fairer terms of trade and increased investment in our economies by the rich nations. This is one sure way in which we can collectively fight poverty through job and wealth creation. In this way, we shall entrench justice and peace which can only be guaranteed when all our people in both rural and urban areas enjoy a reasonable standard of living. As Pope Paul the sixth stated in his encyclical letter, **Populorum Progressio,** *"development is the new name for peace".*

In his New Year address to the Diplomatic Corps accredited to the Vatican on 7th January, 2008: the Holy Father, Pope Benedict the sixteenth, said:

"Peace cannot be a mere word or a vain aspiration. Peace is a commitment and a manner of life which demands that legitimate aspirations of all should be satisfied, such as access to food, water and energy, to medicine and technology, or indeed the monitoring of climate change. Only in this way can we build the future of humanity; only in this way can we facilitate an integral development valid for today and tomorrow ... hence, in order to consolidate peace, the positive macroeconomic results achieved by many developing countries during 2007 must be supported by effective social policies and by the implementation of aid commitments by rich nations".

In concluding my remarks, let me appeal to the Catholic Church, and indeed other churches, to prioritise the attainment of the Millennium Development Goals in your evangelisation and implementation of the social teachings. Let

Appendix 2

us work together, church and state, towards the economic emancipation of all our people through various empowerment initiatives. I am aware, Your Graces, My Lord Bishops, that we all yearn for the integral development of mankind, made especially of body and soul. Our collective challenge, therefore, is to meet both the spiritual and material needs of the people we are privileged to serve. As we pursue our common agenda in this regard, let us be mindful of the need for justice and peace which can only come about through reconciliation. I wish you well in your deliberations. It is my humble prayer that this AMECEA plenary being held in Zambia, will serve as a catalyst in your quest to do better for mankind made in the image and likeness of God.

May the Lord Almighty richly bless your work and life of service to others. It is now my honour and privilege to declare the sixteenth AMECEA plenary assembly under the theme *"Reconciliation through justice and peace"* formally open.

May God bless Zambia.

May God bless Africa.

May God bless the Church.

I thank you.

APPENDIX 3:

MWANAWASA'S FAREWELL SPEECH RECORDED ON 23 MARCH 2005, BROADCAST ON NATIONAL RADIO AND TELEVISION ON 4 SEPTEMBER 2008

It is my wish that this will is broadcast both on television and radio. I now want to address the nation.

I am grateful to all of you for giving me the opportunity during part of my life to serve you as president. It was a privilege which I cherished up to my death. I did all my best to improve the standards of living of you my people. I strove to attend to the production of sufficient food for domestic consumption and for export. I worked hard to encourage investments, both local and foreign, so as to create jobs and so as to enhance the growth of our economy.

I believed that national development could only be sustained if good governance, respect for the rule of law and democracy were encouraged and not taken for granted. To spur these virtues, the fight against corruption had to be waged relentlessly and without treating anybody as a sacred cow.

I regret that in my zeal to facilitate this fight, I lost friendship with a number of some of my best friends and at many times my own life and that of my family members were threatened. I want to assure the nation that no malice or ill will was intended in these initiatives.

I was driven purely by love for my country and the urgent need to transform it from poverty to prosperity. I have always been grieved to see so much poverty, hopelessness and anguish in the faces of our children, the leaders of tomorrow. It has always been my belief that nobody has the right to take away what we should be giving to these children and keep them in their selfish pockets.

I do hope that the party, the Movement for Multiparty Democracy, can continue with this vision for our nation pursuing the fight of zero tolerance to corruption.

I was sad when some of you our members appeared to embrace corruption and actually criticized me for fighting the scourge. This vice will not develop our country. It is my desire that all future governments will continue to wage this fight.

If in my endeavors to provide only the best for my country I offended some of my compatriots, all I can ask is that they should find a place in their hearts to forgive me as no deliberate intentions to harm their feelings without just cause was intended.

To those who attended my funeral and to those who mourned with my family, I say I am extremely grateful to all of you. I am certain that I speak on behalf of my family that their burden has thereby been lightened.

In witness whereof, I, the said Levy Patrick Mwanawasa have hereto set my hand this 23rd day of March, 2005 and I have signed this will as my last will in the presence of my two chief personal secretaries: Brandina Nyendwa and Josephine Shakabinga.

Both of them present at the same time who, at my request, in my presence and in the presence of each of them have subscribed their names as witnesses to the original will which is kept by my bank.

Thank you.

SELECTED BIBLIOGRAPHY

Agyeman-Duah, Baffour (2003). *Managing Leadership Succession in African Politics.* Ghana International Management & Leadership Development Research Institute: Accra.

Annan, K (2012). *Interventions: A Life in War and Peace.* Penguin Books: London.

Chibesakunda, Mwelwa (2001). *The Parliament of Zambia.* National Assembly of Zambia: Lusaka.

Chitala, Mbita (2002). *Not Yet Democracy.* Zambia Research Foundation: Lusaka.

Davoodi, Hamid and Tanzi, Vito (1997). Corruption, Public Investment and Growth, *IMF Working Paper No. 97/139.* [Online]. Retrieved from: http://www.imf.org/external/pubs/ft/wp/wp97139.pdf

Economic Reports (various). Ministry of Finance and National Planning: Lusaka.

Electoral Commission of Zambia. Presidential Election Results. Lusaka.

Fifth National Development Plan and Vision 2030 (2007). Ministry of Finance and National Planning: Lusaka.

Gould, Jeremy. *Democracy and Elections.* Nordic Africa Institute, Number 1, January 2007

Joint Assistance Strategy for Zambia (2007-2010).Ministry of Finance: Lusaka.

Konga, Kenneth (2007). Ministerial Statement to Parliament (Parliament Website: www.parliament.gov.zm).

Matibini, Patrick (2007). *Constitution making Processes: The Case of Zambia.* [Online]. Retrieved from: http://www.osisa.org/resources/docs/PDFs/OpenSpace-June2008/2_2_pp078-92_patrick_matibini_constitution-making.pdf

Mbao, Melvin Y (2007). *The Politics of Constitution – Making in Zambia: Where Does The Constituent Power Lie?* [Online]. Retrieved from: http://www.enelsyn.gr/papers/w1/Paper%20by%20Prof.%20Melvin%20L%20M%20Mbao.pdf

Meredith, Martin (2005). *The State of Africa: A History of Fifty Years of Independence.* Simon & Schuster Publishers.

MMD Constitution (2001). MMD Secretariat: Lusaka

Moyo, Dambisa (2009) *Dead Aid. Why Aid Is Not Working and How There Is Another Way For Africa.* Penguin Group Publishers: London

Musakanya, Valentine (2010). *The Musakanya Papers: The Autobiographical Writings of Valentine Musakaya.* Lembani Trust: Lusaka

Mwaanga, Vernon J (2008). *The Long Sunset.* Fleetfoot Publishing Company: Lusaka

Mwanakatwe, John (1994). *End of Kaunda Era.* Multimedia Publications: Lusaka

National Budgets (various). Ministry of Finance and National Planning: Lusaka

National Decentralisation Policy 2005. Ministry of Local Government and Housing: Lusaka

National Governance Baseline Survey, (2004). Ministry of Justice: Lusaka

NCC Act Number 19 of 2007. Government Printers: Lusaka

Powell, C. (1995). *My American Journey*. Random House Publishing Group: New York.

Presidential Petition Judgment (2005). Supreme Court of Zambia: Lusaka

Report of the National Commission on the Establishment of a One-Party Participatory Democracy in Zambia (1972). [Online]. Retrieved from: http://www.unza.zm/zamlii/downloads/chona-report.pdf

Russell, Alec (2010). *After Mandela*. Windmill Books: London.

Sakala, Richard L (2009). *A Mockery of Justice*. Sentor Publishers: Lusaka

Tanzi, V and Davoodi, H (1997). *Corruption, Public Investment and Growth*. International Monetary Fund: Washington.

Transparency International Zambia, Opinion Poll on Lusaka Residents' Perceptions of Corruption (2005). [Online]. Retrieved from: http://www.tizambia.org.zm/download/uploads/OPINION_POLL_ON_LUSAKA_RESIDENTS_PERCEPTIONS_OF_CORRUPTION.pdf

United Nations Congress on the Prevention of Crime and Treatment of Offenders. [Online]. Retrieved from: http://www.un.org/events/10thcongress/2088b.htm

World Bank (2012). *Corruption from the Perspective of Citizens, Firms, and Public Officials - Results of Sociological Surveys*. National Political Publishing House: Hanoi

Zambia Privatisation Agency Study, (2005). Lusaka

Speeches
Presidential Address to the Nation, 4 May, 2001

Presidential Address to the Nation, 17 April, 2003

Newspapers

Zambia Daily Mail, 25 January, 2007

Times of Zambia, 1 October, 2007

Times of Zambia, 10 October, 2006

The Post, 13 July, 2002

The Post, 3 April, 2007

The Post, 26 September, 2010

www.ingramcontent.com/pod-product-compliance
Lightning Source LLC
Chambersburg PA
CBHW070830300426
44111CB00014B/2511